S0-AHK-144

Also by Neil M. Kay

THE INNOVATING FIRM: A Behavioural Theory of Corporate
R & D

THE EVOLVING FIRM

Traditionally, economics has been concerned with single firms and consumers. The firm, the industry and the economy are interpreted as the sum of their respective parts. In this approach the basic building blocks must be treated as individual elements and highly unrealistic assumptions made to create a rigorous theory.

However, this approach has encountered severe problems in dealing with the behaviour of the modern corporation. Why has the post-war period been characterized by the growth of large, diversified corporations in most developed countries? Why are some industries characterized by highly specialized corporate strategies while others are occupied by giant conglomerates? What are the reasons behind the post-war merger wave, takeovers and the move towards increased overall concentration? Traditional analysis has encountered profound difficulties in dealing with these questions.

Instead of taking the single product-market as the basis for analysis *The Evolving Firm* considers these questions by looking at the concepts of links and relationships *between* product-markets, an approach not possible in traditional analysis. Techniques for mapping the strategy of the corporation are developed and related to questions of hierarchy. This novel theory builds from a simple model to analyze problems of diversification merger, takeover, aggregate concentration and internal organization.

While Neil M. Kay looks at problems of industrial organization, he also offers a framework which will prove useful in the business policy area.

Neil M. Kay is a graduate of Stirling University and was a Lecturer at Nottingham and Strathclyde Universities before taking up his present position of Lecturer in Industrial Economics at Heriot-Watt University, Edinburgh. He was visiting Associate Professor at the University of California, Irvine, in the Economics Department, 1980–1, and in the Graduate School of Management, 1981–2.

THE EVOLVING FIRM
Strategy and Structure in Industrial Organization

Neil M. Kay

St. Martin's Press   New York

203476

658.402
K 23

© Neil M. Kay 1982

All rights reserved. For information, write:
St. Martin's Press, Inc., 175 Fifth Avenue, New York, NY 10010
Printed in Hong Kong
First published in the United States of America in 1982

ISBN 0–312–27316–9

Library of Congress Cataloging in Publication Data

Kay, Neil M.
 The evolving firm.

 Bibliography: p.
 Includes index.
 1. Industrial organization. 2. Industrial
management. 3. Corporations—Management. I.
Title.
HD31.K35   1982   658.4′02   81-21436
ISBN 0–312–27316–9   AACR2

To Betty, Jack and Gret

Contents

Preface

This work is concerned with the economic behaviour of the large modern corporation. It is intended as a contribution both to the theory of the firm and to the field of industrial organisation. This broad area has been the subject of intense activity on both theoretical and empirical fronts in recent years, but in general results have not been encouraging. Despite a proliferation of theories of the firm too many major issues and problems in industrial organisation have not been satisfactorily dealt with for economic analysis to be judged successful up to this point.

The starting-point for this work is the suggestion that the basic reason for this unsatisfactory state of affairs is fundamental weakness in the central assumptions of the theory of the firm. If the arguments of this book are correct, it is ironic that the problem was correctly specified and an alternative approach suggested as long ago as the 1930s by R. H. Coase. Coase argued that firms existed because of transaction costs of market exchange. Coase's paper became generally recognised as providing a rationale for the corporation, but until recently its influence was limited. Textbooks in the area would frequently base their first chapter on Coase's explanation of the nature of the firm, and then proceed effectively to ignore information problems in subsequent chapters by reducing the problem of the behaviour of firms to exercises in neoclassical price-setting.

What was generally overlooked with respect to Coase's analysis was that it not only explained why firms existed in the first place, but also provided a basis for analysing the determinants of the boundaries of the firm – firm co-ordination supplanted market exchange when management costs were less than transaction costs. If transaction cost analysis can explain the boundaries of the firm, it should be able to deal with such problems as vertical integration, diversification, merger, takeover and size of firm, all of which involve the extent or the extension of the boundaries of the firm.

In the 1970s the potential relevance of transaction cost analysis to the problem of vertical integration was recognised by O. E.

Williamson and applied by him in a number of papers and his book *Markets and Hierarchies* (1975). I suggest here that this approach can be extended to cover other important problems of resource allocation in the area of industrial organisation.

In addition to transaction cost analysis there is a second major theoretical perspective underlying this work: structuralism. Structuralism is a paradigm which has been subjected to a variety of interpretations in the social sciences, though I select a limited and, I hope, consistent view of it here.

The two approaches, transaction cost analysis and structuralism, are presented here as complementary perspectives which can be usefully combined within one theoretical framework. Since most works are generally content with one theoretical approach, I might be reasonably expected to justify the complication of adding a second. If the approach works, this is sufficient justification. If the reader does not feel that the approach works then I would be tempted to adopt a more ignoble defence and blame my colleague Geoff Wyatt for asking a central question at a departmental seminar given by me at Heriot-Watt University. I had used the concept of synergy in some earlier versions of this work, and Geoff Wyatt raised the issue of whether or not synergy could be traded. This encouraged me to reappraise the approach in the light of transaction cost analysis.

Since the final draft of this book was prepared, I have discovered what I believe may be interpreted as an independent development of the principle of trading synergy gains. D. J. Teece (1980) argues that Williamson's transaction cost analysis can be applied to the issue of economies of scope. Since at a formal level I argue here that economies of scope and synergy are equivalent, Teece's article effectively represents a separate development of the concept of synergy trading in the context of transaction cost analysis. However, Teece argues that economies of scope cannot provide a satisfactory basis for a theory of diversification. I argue here that it can, once it is married with the concept of environmental threat.

I am, of course, grateful to Geoff Wyatt for his help and also to my colleagues Peter Clarke, Philip Welham and Les Simpson for their advice and encouragement. John Scouller at Strathclyde University drew my attention to related works by Buckley and Casson on multinational enterprise; while it was too late to develop the link in this work, it is a promising area for future study. I have also benefited from discussion at other seminar presentations I have made at the Universities of Strathclyde, Stirling, Nottingham and California. It is not possible to thank each contributor individually, but I am especially grateful to Peter Earle, Johnnie Johnstone, Brian Loasby, Bob Hamilton, Peter McGregor and Charlie Lave.

In addition, the academic years from 1979 to 1981 gave me an opportunity to try the synergy mapping approach as a teaching tool at the Universities of Heriot-Watt and California. The response was encouraging and the ideas were generally treated as both natural and obvious by the students – which may or may not be a good thing.

Students at both Universities provided useful comments and work on the ideas but Brian Crawford, Jo-Ellen Thompson, Joel Walker, Stephanie Smith and Bob Albright merit special attention.

I am also grateful to Pat Lean, Jean Roberts and Rosemary Johnson for their cheerful and invaluable assistance in typing the manuscript.

N. M. K.

Acknowledgements

I am grateful for permission to reproduce the following tables and figures. Tables 6.1, 7.1 and 7.2 from Richard Rumelt, *Strategy, Structure and Economic Performance* (Harvard Business School, 1974). Table 6.4 from R. R. Nelson, J. J. Peck, and E. D. Kalachek, *Technology, Economic Growth and Public Policy* (Washington, Brookings Institution, 1967). Figures 7.1 and 7.4 from J. W. H. Clare, 'Current Trends in the Organization of Industrial Research', *Research Management*, 1963, 7, 393–406. Figure 7.4 from S. Prais, *The Evolution of Giant Firms in Britain* (London, National Institute of Economic and Social Research). Table 7.4 from A. Wood, 'Organization, Merger and Research Expenditures: a Review of Empirical Studies', in R. Marris and A. Wood (eds), *The Corporate Economy: Growth, Competition and Innovative Potential* (London, Macmillan) pp. 428–53.

1 Introduction

The following analysis is offered as a contribution to the theory of the firm and as a method of analysing some problems in industrial organisation. It draws on ideas and material from economics and related disciplines and attempts to synthesise and develop these diverse sources into a useful framework. It must be admitted that in many cases insights and interpretations provided by other social sciences proved more useful than what was available in economic analysis; though only cursory treatment and recognition of these contributions is possible here, they have proved invaluable in providing direction and perspective for the present work. Recently, however, there are indications that new approaches to old problems in microtheory may have real potential for industrial organisation issues, and these are heavily relied on in subsequent chapters.

   The limited usefulness of existing economic theory is felt here to have a major root cause, and that is the dominating position of perfect competition in this area. This may appear a surprising claim in the light of the appearance of many novel and distinctive theories of the firm in recent years, yet perfect competition still exerts a pervasive influence. The influence of perfect competition is both direct and indirect; not only is it still recognised as a useful or convenient approach in many areas, but it also commonly represents the point of departure for the development of alternative theories.[1] Thus, many recent theories of the firm represent marginal developments of perfect competition in which one or two assumptions have been modified. There are strong kinship relationships between many contemporary theories of the firm due to their common ancestor, perfect competition; and the great grand-daddy of them all is still alive though signs of senility have been widely commented on.

   Such a family tree of economic theories is not necessarily a bad thing. However, this close relationship between theories carries with it the potential danger that the apparent differences between theories obscures the inappropriateness of the common family traits they exhibit. This is in fact the stance adopted here, and will be argued in

1

later chapters. For the moment we will restrict ourselves in this chapter to briefly recapping the main developments in the theory of the firm family. We shall later argue that these theories tend to be based on unsuitable building blocks for many of the areas they are applied to. It will be suggested that a fundamental rethinking of the theory of the firm is required, and that the tools for redesign are already available. The requisite materials are scattered in a number of sources inside and outside economics and will be introduced in the course of the analysis where appropriate.[2]

THE THEORY OF THE FIRM

Until the 1930s the perfectly competitive theory of the firm represented the basic interpretation of the role of firm in economic theory. Monopoly and oligopoly theories existed, but were seen to be of peripheral concern to economists. The general theory of the firm was perfect competition, with monopoly and oligopoly representing occasional special cases.

However, perfect competition was a means to an end in the early days of the theory of the firm, and that end was general equilibrium theory. The assumptions of perfect competition allow the innards of the firm to be ignored and facilitate the development of a theory of value in which overall allocative efficiency and income distribution could be studied easily.[3] The firm can be regarded as a 'black box' with no discretion over resource allocation questions; the perfect competition rules must be obeyed, or the firm leaves the field. Since the main interest of enquiry was general equilibrium, ability to neglect the firm as a decision-making unit was to the credit of perfect competition, and was convenient. However, determinate solutions were achieved in perfect competition only by assuming that the long run average cost curve eventually turns up. Homogenous replicable inputs and perfect knowledge ensures that the only reason for an upturn in the long run average cost curve is eventual rise in input prices.

This line of argument was developed by Sraffa (1926) to demonstrate that perfect competition was not reconcilable with partial equilibrium. If input prices rise, they will affect the demand curve of the supplying industry and the cost curves of other industries using this input; *ceteris paribus* does not hold, and we are faced with a general equilibrium problem, not a partial equilibrium problem. Firms and industries cannot be studied independently of other firms and industries.

The result of Sraffa's analysis was to stimulate investigation into possible escape routes out of this impasse. Imperfect or monopolistic competition (associated with the names of Robinson (1933) and Chamberlin (1933) respectively) suggested one resolution of the problem by permitting the retention of declining cost curves (and so partial equilibrium analysis) by introducing the concept of declining demand curves for firms competing in the same industry or group. While severe methodological criticisms have been made of this development, it still represented an attempt to maintain a partial equilibrium approach to resource allocation at the level of the firm.

The stimulus for the development of monopolistic/imperfect competition was the desire for elegance expressed as an integrated and self-consistent theory having determinate solutions. Theoretical rigour took precedence over empirical relevance. However, even on its own terms monopolistic/imperfect competition must be judged a failure since subsequent scrutiny has illuminated serious inconsistencies in both approaches; Loasby (1976, pp. 173–92) concludes after detailed examination of Chamberlin and Robinson's approaches that 'imperfect competition depends on irrationality, monopolistic competition is internally self-contradictory'. (p. 183). While such defects may be wounding to theories which have some empirical standing, they are potentially fatal flaws in the case of theories which have rigour as their primary goal.

However, one aspect of this work which is of fundamental importance to the development of the theory of the firm is identified by Shackle (1967):

Mrs Robinson starts her first chapter with a strangely revealing sentence: The purpose of this book is to demonstrate that the analysis of the output and price of a single commodity can be conducted by a technique based upon the study of individual decisions. The individual decisions were those of the entrepreneur or his firm and each of the commodities whose prices and outputs were in question was defined, not as a stuff having given physical characteristics, but as the product of a particular firm. Primacy had passed from the autonomously self-subsisting technical commodity to the firm considered as a profit-maximising policy maker. (p. 65)

In attempting to rescue a partial equilibrium approach, the firm emerged as a decision-making unit in its own right. Even if the theory of imperfect competition was not a success, it set the context for subsequent developments in the theory of the firm. The perfect competition role for the firm as a black-box began to be questioned with these modifications.

Subsequent major theoretical developments took some time to appear and hindsight allows us to classify them into two main categories: managerial and behavioural theories. Managerial theories may be regarded as having their original stimulus in a work contemporary with Robinson's and Chamberlin's publications; Berle and Means' (1932) analysis of the separation of ownership from control of the large corporation. The absence of tight market or shareholder discipline on management decision-making enables discretion to be exercised by the latter group in pursuit of their own objectives. Notable contributions in this area include constrained sales maximisation (Baumol, 1959), constrained growth maximisation (Marris, 1963, 1966) and constrained utility maximisation (Williamson, 1964). Each of these is built on the assumptions that the motive for the pursuit of non-profit objectives exists (provided by the separation of ownership and control) and that the opportunity for the pursuit of these objectives exists (provided by favourable environmental conditions affording managerial discretion).

Like imperfect/monopolist competition, managerial theories may be regarded as evolving from preceding neoclassical theory[4] rather than presenting a radically different perspective. The constrained maximisation approach is retained, only the objectives pursued differ. Indeed, the similarity of the theoretical base of both neoclassical theory and managerial theory generally permits qualitative comparisons of resource allocation issues in the respective approaches. However, managerial theory does differ significantly from imperfect and monopolistic competition in terms of its origins; while the former sought legitimacy through its attempts to refine an impure theory, managerial theory represents a response to a problem with empirical origins. As such it represents one step forward for the theory of the firm in so far as it recognises such problems exist.

Behavioural theory has emerged recently from similar empirical preoccupations. Like managerial theory, it postulates that separation of ownership and control combined with a benign environment leads to the pursuit of managerial objectives. However not only is *profit* maximising abandoned in behavioural theory, so also is the concept of *maximising* itself. The standard work in this area is Cyert and March

(1963) who developed Simon's work (1957). Simon argued that the limited cognitive ability of decision-makers resulted in 'bounded rationality' and effectively precluded maximising when environmental uncertainty existed. Instead individuals 'satisficed' or sought acceptable levels of goals expressed in terms of aspiration levels. The organisation is a coalition of individuals each with their own goals set at aspiration levels which adapt to changes in the environment. Behavioural theory is therefore a theory of short run adaptation in the face of uncertainty, and with managerial discretion over selection of goals. It represents a radical departure from the family tree of neoclassical and managerial theory, and indeed its origins in organisational theory mark it as a creature of an entirely different genus. As far as resource allocation issues are concerned, qualitative comparisons between neoclassical and behavioural theory are inhibited by behavioural theories' emphasis on individual experience and learning in dictating aspiration levels and responses to environmental changes. Decision-making is based on subjective rationality in behavioural theory and contrasts with the unbounded or objective rationality of neoclassical theory.

These represent the major groupings in the theory of the firm at the present time, though other developments warrant mention. Contributions in neoclassical theory have continued to be made, particularly in oligopoly theory[5]. Leibenstein's analysis (1966, 1969, 1973) of the efficiency implications of X- or technical efficiency also represents a significant recent contribution

Each of these approaches represents an attempt to add to our understanding of how resource allocation is carried out at the level of the firm. Depending on circumstances, they attempt to explain or predict how the decisions of the firm are made. In principle, each may be formulated in such a way as to generate potentially refutable propositions. The possibility of empirical testing is essential to claims that such a body of knowledge as economic science exists, and researchers in the area of the theory of firm have not been slow to recognise the entrance qualifications for scientific status in their work.[6] In fact, there are some striking similiarities between physics and the theory of the firm, not only a terms of methodology, but also in terms of content and direction of work. As will be discussed in the next chapter, traditional general equilibrium models are expressed in an analogous fashion to thermodynamic models in physics. Further, Robinson and Chamberlin's search for a rigorous theory of the firm with determinate solutions was conducted at a time when physics was still a science of determinacy and precision.[7] Although Einstein's theory of relativity had revolutionised physics, it was still a theory of determinate and precise solutions. Quantum mechanics and the associated problems of indeterminacy of particle behaviour was at an embryo stage of development and was largely rejected by Einstein, who by this represented the voice of physics establishment to a large extent.[8]

While the procedural aspects of Robinson and Chamberlin's quest found a comforting echo in the general tradition of physics as it stood at that time, in recent years uncertainty has assumed a central role in physics through developments in quantum theory. Heisenberg's 'uncertainty principle', which sets limits to the possibility of measurement of behaviour at the atomic level, challenged the elegance of received physics. Similarly, uncertainty has emerged as a major consideration in economics in recent years; the behavioural theory of the firm was designed with this concept serving as its main foundation.

While it is not suggested here that theorists such as Walras (one of the architects of a formal general equilibrium theory), Robinson, Chamberlin and Simon deliberately adopted the philosophy of conventional physics, it is quite possible that the prevailing atmosphere of contemporary physical science in each case influenced the economic analysis, to a greater or lesser extent. Certainly the desire for scientific status evinced by the economics establishment over succeeding generations would be expected to encourage receptivity to current conventions and ideas in science, whether deliberately or unconsciously. Even the mathematical tools widely adopted by modern microeconomists were crafted and tempered in physics.

However, if economics in general (and the theory of the firm in particular) aspires to the status of a science, it must also expect to be judged by the standards of a science; merely wearing the clothes of physics by mimicking its pursuit of elegant mathematical abstractions is not acceptable. The test of a true science is its ability to explain and predict. How does the theory of the firm perform on this account?

One crude test of what constitutes the dominant paradigm or paradigms is to examine standard texts. The most recent text I have to hand in this area is Koutsoyiannis (1979), a comprehensive textbook on microeconomics at intermediate level. Almost half of the pages are devoted to oligopoly behaviour; in all, about 80 per cent of the book is devoted to neoclassical theory (indifference curves, cost curves, perfect competition, monopoly, monopolistic competition, oligopoly, factor pricing, general equilibrium theory and welfare economics), with the remainder devoted to managerial theory, behavioural theory, theory of games and linear programming. Koutsoyiannis' text represents a fairly typical coverage of received micro-theory, though with a rather heavier emphasis on oligopoly than is normal. The back cover suggests that it equips the student with 'a theoretical framework which will help him approach and analyse with more realism the complex phenomena of the business world'.

While sympathising with the ambition underlying this claim and the implicit appeal it makes to tolerance on the part of students undergoing intermediate economics, in teaching intermediate economics I occasionally suffer pangs of remorse in training students to jump through the hoops of perfect competition, monopoly, monopolistic competition, oligopoly, factor pricing, general equilibrium theory and welfare theory. If any of these approaches were to provide some insight into such basic questions as 'Why ICI?' they would be easier to justify. The alternative justification – that they provide good analytical training – is reminiscent of the pursuit of rigour for rigour's sake in the 1930s. It is tempting to persuade students that intermediate economics is an unpleasant pill to be swallowed before the revelation of the full empirical power of the theory of the firm at a later date; but it is a fallacy.

In later chapters it will be suggested that received theory has limited scope and does not deal adequately with central problems of resource allocation at corporate level in the economy. It will be argued that the reasons for this failure are attributable to the make up of the theory itself; there is something flawed in the state of economic theory that proves an obstruction to empirical analysis. The flaw is identified as being the technique of aggregation, and an alternative perspective is developed that may prove helpful in the analysis of such problems.

This is not to suggest that neoclassical theory is of no relevance; rather it is argued that it has been overstretched in being applied to inappropriate levels of analysis. It is hoped that the following chapters will help to indicate how an alternative approach may be built up.

PLAN OF THE BOOK

The argument is presented in three stages; context, theory and empirical analysis. There is a movement from the abstract to the concrete in the course of the book that is particularly noticeable as we progress from one stage to another. The context is set out in Chapter 2. In this section the concept of structuralism is introduced and discussed with particular emphasis on its application in other social sciences. The essence of the structuralist approach may be said to be anti-aggregation; in contrast to neoclassical theory whose technique of aggregation is based on the assumption of independence and separability of constituent elements in the analysis, structuralism is concerned with the implications of interdependency and links between the observed elements. Neither approach should be regarded as innately superior, since whether aggregation or structuralism is of greater potential relevance depends on the phenomena under examination. If observation suggests separability of components is a reasonable assumption then aggregation provides a simple method of analysis. On the other hand, if it appears that there exists significant interdependency, a structuralist approach may be more appropriate.

Therefore Chapter 2 outlines a potentially useful alternative to aggregation that has been widely applied in the other social sciences. The function of the chapter is that of description of possibilities; no attempt is made here to argue that structuralism is automatically a suitable approach for economic analysis. The chapter is merely concerned with delineating territorial boundaries for the subsequent discussion.

The second stage of the analysis is concerned with the development of a theoretical base and covers Chapters 3, 4 and 5. While structuralism indicates the direction in which theory building should proceed, the task of theory building must be related to the problem under discussion. Consequently, the three chapters concerned with theory development adopt a structuralist perspective to the specific demands of the theory of the firm and industrial organisation. To start with, Chapter 3 concerns itself with the problems of why and how firms exist; why firms exist is attributable to transaction costs, while how firms exist involves hierarchy and synergy. This latter concept refers to links between product markets and will be developed as a central structuralist element in our argument. We shall argue here that synergy relationships within firms evolve from transaction cost considerations and also introduce the idea of synergy mapping as an aid to analysis.

Chapter 4 continues the theme of theory development and starts by relating the present analysis to that of Kay (1979). Both works have structuralist roots and the argument of Chapter 2 is useful in helping to compare and contrast the respective approaches. The chapter also integrates hierarchy and synergy maps and shows how the latter can be related to choice of internal organisation. Here also product life cycles are introduced into the discussion and analysed as a tool of corporate strategy.

I believe the most interesting aspect of this part of the work is that it combines four distinctive and familiar concepts in a novel and potentially useful framework. Transaction cost analysis (from economic theory), hierarchy or internal organisation (from organisation theory), and synergy and product life cycles (from the business policy/corporate strategy literature) all play essential and complementary roles in the framework. The selective nature of this construction would have been a potential source of weakness if a marriage of incompatibles had been attempted; it is hoped to show that – in this context as least – polygamy works.

While Chapters 3 and 4 set up the building blocks, Chapter 5 attempts to develop a formal theory on these foundations. Having established our framework in Chapters 3 and 4 there are two directions subsequent analysis could take. One fork leads to a case by case examination of business policy using synergy maps, while the other fork leads to more abstract formal modelling of resource allocation problems. In this work we choose the second fork and pursue resource allocation questions, leaving aside detailed analysis of business policy questions for the moment.

The latter part of the book is concerned with the third stage, that of empirical analysis. In Chapter 6 we attempt to account for patterns of industrial diversification by using the model developed in Chapter 5. Existing studies of diversification are re-appraised in the light of the framework developed here. In particular, a number of studies testing technical skills and portfolio risk theories of diversification are scrutinised and their conclusions reconsidered. It is suggested that the model developed here is particularly useful in helping to reconcile some apparent inconsistencies and puzzles in the literature.

The empirical analysis shifts in Chapter 7 to consider the related topics of aggregate concentration and direction of merger. The reasons for changes in aggregate concentration are identified as resulting from changes in corporate strategy. Mergers are an important aspect of this process, and the centrality of environmental technological change as a determinant of merger and aggregate concentration is highlighted in this chapter.

Chapter 8 continues along the empirical path, but differs from the previous two chapters in that no new analysis or re-interpretation of existing studies is provided. Instead, the purpose of the chapter is to extend discussion of strategy and structure to show how our framework can satisfactorily integrate both these aspects.

Finally, Chapter 9 ties some threads together and suggests implications for future analysis. The approach can be developed in a number of ways, and this chapter attempts no more than a brief survey of possibilities.

The overall objective is to develop a structuralist approach to the theory of the firm and to see if it is useful. Usefulness is the first requisite of a good theory, and tentatively it is to be hoped that the ensuing analysis can be regarded as giving grounds for optimism in this respect.

First, however, we shall give further consideration to the question of economics as science in the next chapter. We shall argue that the rules of the game in economics are generally based on an overly restricted interpretation of what constitutes legitimate scientific theorising, and that one paradigm in particular that has been applied with some success in other social sciences offers genuine opportunity for worthwhile revisionism in economic theorising.

2 Systems and Structure

As emphasised in Chapter 1, this work is concerned with the way we look at economic behaviour. In this respect, generations of novel developments in economic theory building have developed an ability to portray and interpret the world in an impressive variety of perspectives. The theory of the firm is one arena in which the near gymnastic agility of economic analysis has been well exercised. Assuming adequate data, a microeconomist should be capable of analysing a given market or industry using perfect competition, monopolistic competition, monopoly, oligopoly,[1] utility maximising, sales revenue maximising, behavioural, M-Form and X-efficiency theories of the firm. The result is the theory of the firm has developed a decathlete's all round facility for dealing with empirical exercises.

However, an interesting aspect of this gymnasium is that price is no longer a solo performer. In neoclassical theory, problems of resource allocation were virtually synonymous with price determination. In the new theories of the firm the role of price is usually less central and its relevance for resource allocation less clear cut. In particular behavioural and managerial theories have identified other determinants of resource allocation.

In principle, at least, the central problem of resource allocation is kept firmly in mind in the new theories. In practice the questionable status of price has dimmed the ability of theory of the firm to make market, industry or economy level statements with respect to resource allocation. In neoclassical theory the step from firm to industry was typically a trivial one involving simple aggregation. In firms were not homogenous to start with, pursuit of profit homogenised them. However, variety and heterogeneity in resource allocation are a direct consequence of slack market discipline in the new theories of the firm. If managerial theories permit discretion in the choice of objectives, what is to constrain one firm's objectives to be the same as another? If behavioural theory emphasises experience in the formulation of decision rules and aspiration levels, how can we do other than study firms as unique systems? The 'representative firm' is an obsolete

11

concept. This problem has been recognised in connection with behavioural theory,[2] but is has wider scope than that. Not surprisingly the new theories of the firm have tended to be restricted to the corporate system rather than extended to industry or economy level.

Up to a point, this poses no problem. The firm is interesting in its own right, and studies of individual firms may be a useful and rewarding exercise without wider considerations necessarily being involved. However there are dangers in indulging in such developments which have been well recognised by the neoclassical theorists. How can we make statements about the general pattern of resource allocation in the economy as a whole with the self imposed myopia resulting from the new theories of the firm? Our extensions of the theory of the firm begin to look like contractions in its scope and generality. Do we abandon the search for a contribution to systematic explanation of microeconomic behaviour a level above that of the individual firm, or do we have to adopt highly abstract and ill-fitting theoretical approaches as a necessary cost of generality?

The difficulties of systematic explanation appear to be reinforced when we observe the apparent diversity and irregularity of corporate behaviour and types in the modern economy. It could be argued that some of the most interesting resource allocation questions are to be asked at this level. Why do we observe differences between firms in terms of diversification? What causes changes in aggregate concentration? Why do some firms adopt entrenched vertically integrated strategies? What implications does technological change have for resource allocation?

The desirability of identification of patterns at this level is an obvious stimulus to the development of the theory of the firm. Neoclassical theory had the potential range to deal with questions posed at this level. Yet, as will be discussed further later, neoclassical theory is not capable of adequately dealing with the major resource allocation questions of the corporate economy. The new theories of the firm have added internal factors to the theory of the firm, but this very contribution has limited their generality.

It may be that it is impossible to develop simple, general theories that provide a useful description of patterns of resource allocation. A more optimistic viewpoint is adopted here. It is believed there is genuine scope for the development of theory in this area. In the remainder of this chapter we shall discuss the foundations of the approach to be applied in later chapters. In this connection the theoretical approaches of the psychologist Piaget, the social anthropologist Lévi-Strauss and the psycholinguist Chomsky will be referred to briefly. It will be argued that the structuralist perspectives they have applied in their respective fields may provide useful insights for the building of economic theories.

However, before we look at these approaches some further comment is appropriate. Firstly, we shall be concerned with the procedure followed by each analyst looked at below, rather than with detailed analysis of the substance and content of their respective areas. There are strong similarities in the frameworks used by Piaget, Chomsky and Lévi-Strauss which are relatively easy to identify compared to the complexity and depth embodied in the detailed arguments and analysis of their respective works. We hope to show that it is possible to gain an elementary understanding of similarities in the analytical tools employed by the respective theorists without having to attain professional competence in psychology, linguistics and anthropology.

Secondly, a plea for tolerance on the part of the reader is made. Four main terms are introduced in this chapter that are liable to be novel to economists – analytical and global structuralism, synchronic and diachronic relations. This jargon is introduced as a means to an end rather than as an end in itself. The working rule for jargon is: does it summarise and explain a critical concept such that it does not have to be re-explained every time in enters an argument? I believe the concepts introduced here do perform such a useful function, and that they will be of assistance in helping to discriminate between alternative theoretical standpoints in later analysis. It is hoped that economists of a nervous or sensitive disposition will have the patience to sit out this phase of the analysis.

With these riders in mind, we shall use Piaget's (1968) analysis as a basis for comparing theoretical frameworks. Piaget chooses to categorise approaches into three main types each of which has distinctive characteristics associated with them. We shall find each type of direct relevance in our later analysis.

Piaget makes a distinction between aggregates and structures (1968, p.7) and between what he describes as 'analytic' and 'global' structuralism as applied in the social sciences (1968, pp.97–9). These distinctions provide a sound basis for identifying significant features of alternative theoretical standpoints.[3] We shall use Piaget's distinctions and examine each approach in turn.

AGGREGATION

Piaget defines aggregates as 'composites formed of elements that are independent of the complexes into which they enter' (1968, p.7). At first sight this seems entirely consistent with aggregation as used in economic analysis. The conventional economic approach[4] is to first isolate building blocks (individual products and consumers) using which higher level systems are described; the behaviour of groups is treated as an aggregative phenomenon, e.g.

$$Q_I = \sum_{i=1}^{n} q_i$$

where Q_I = industry output
q_i = ith firm in industry, $i = 1 \ldots$ n.

Aggregation forms the basis of the distinction between microeconomics and macroeconomics, the latter utilising aggregations of microeconomic elements in its analysis. However aggregation is also used in examination of intermediate systems; for example analysis of market structures is based on the concept of the modern corporation as the sum total of individual products and their markets.

FIGURE 2.1   Aggregation

Piaget's definition can also be illustrated diagrammatically, as in Fig. 2.1. This illustrates two elements having no relationship or interaction between them. The composite can be simply analysed as the sum total of the characteristics of the two elements. If the two elements are both one pence pieces, the composite is twopence.

Up to this point there appears little difficulty. However, we can introduce a problem by picking up the argument in a previous work (Kay 1979, pp.210–11) at almost the point at which the work concluded. The discussion here concerned itself with a debate in which Vining (1949) argued that aggregation could distort representation of composites. Koopmans (1949) could not accept this; Vining's comment is quoted in Koopmans' rejoinder:

I cannot understand the meaning of the phrase that the 'aggregate has an existence apart from its constituent particles and behaviour characteristics of its own not deducible from the behaviour characteristics of the particles'. If a theory formulates precisely (although possibly in probability terms) the determination of the choices and actions of each individual in a group or population, in response to the choices and actions of other individuals or the consequences thereof (such as prices, quantities, state of expectation) then the set of these individually behaviour characteristics is *logically* equivalent to the behaviour characteristics of the group. (Koopmans, 1949, p.86–7)

While Koopmans' statement raises other issues which were discussed in Kay (1979, Chapter 9), one aspect of Koopmans' interpretation of the nature of aggregates is particularly noteworthy here. Koopmans states that the aggregate may be defined as being equivalent to the set of individual characteristics of constituent elements, with inter-relationships between these elements being permitted. On the other hand, we have seen that Piaget stresses the absence of inter-relationships between elements composing an aggregate. We have conflicting interpretations of the concept. While it might be tempting to suggest that such inconsistency is not important, this would be almost irresponsible; as has been mentioned above, to a large extent economics *is* aggregation. Bypassing this point could obscure an issue of genuine importance.

It will be argued that in fact both definitions may be valid descriptions of aggregation in economics, and that the difference between them illuminates an important aspect of the role of aggregation.

General equilibrium theory poses the severest test of Piaget's definition and appears perfectly consistent with Koopmans, and so we shall analyse aggregation in this context. As Baumol (1965) points out:

General equilibrium theory was developed to take account of a cardinal feature of the structure of our economy: the interdependence of its parts. A rise in the price of automobiles can reduce the demand for tires and increase the demand for bus transportation. A rise in wages may increase imports, reduce exports, and increase the use of labor-saving machinery. The set of examples can be expanded indefinitely. (p.338)

Inter-relatedness of markets is a basic construct of general equilibrium theory. For example, for an economy with m goods (including money), we might write the demand for the jth good as follows:

$$D_j = f(P_1 \ldots P_m, W, M) \qquad j = 1 \ldots m$$

where P_j is the price of the jth good, W is stock of wealth, M is stock of cash. Demand for the jth good is dependent on the price of all other goods, and the stocks of wealth and cash in the economy. However, despite this, aggregation is still a basic operation in general equilibrium theory, e.g. Walras' Law:

$$\sum_{j=1}^{M} P_j S_j \equiv \sum_{j=1}^{M} P_j D_j$$

where S_j is supply of jth good. Walras' Law states that total money value of all items supplied must equal total money value of all items demanded. Two aspects merit emphasis in Walras' law – we use aggregation, and the identity takes no account of possible relationships between constituent elements.

One way of analysing how this is possible is to pose a simple question; what happens when all aspects of *time* are removed from general equilibrium analysis? That is, how is our system affected when it is reduced to a completely static state?

The answer is that the interdependencies disappear from the system. The relationships in general equilibrium theory are specified in *adjustment* terms, whether this is explicit as in dynamic analysis, or implicit as in comparative statics. The quotation above by Baumol contains an example of how such adjustment relationships may be expressed in comparative static terms. In dynamic analysis the process of *tatonnement* by a ghostly auctioneer allows adjustment of contracts to take place until equilibrium is achieved. If we have a perfectly static world we eliminate the possibility of adjustment, which in turn eliminates the relevance of relationships expressed in adjustment terms, which means we can treat the system as an aggregate in Piaget's sense of the term. The price system consists of price signals or *guides to movement*. Just as traffic signals are redundant in a traffic jam, so the relationships implied in price signals disappear in a static world. Thus, both Koopmans' and Piaget's definitions of aggregation are valid depending on which aspect of the problem we are studying at the time. In this context, it is worthwhile noting that Loasby (1976, p.46) compares comparative static general equilibrium approaches to thermodynamic equilibrium models. This is a useful illustration of the properties of general equilibrium; if we have a simple gas like oxygen (O_2) then adjustments to equilibrium conditions of pressure and temperature are determined by the laws of thermo*dynamics*. Removal of the dynamic element means oxygen molecules can be treated as isolates and aggregated to describe the larger system.

As far as specific theories of market structure are concerned, oligopoly is the neoclassical approach which specifically recognises interdependencies between individual firms. Here again the interdependencies are expressed on an adjustment basis, usually in terms of firms' reactions to other firms' actions. Eliminating the dynamic element again eliminates the interdependencies and permits aggregation.

So we have described how an aggregate in the perfectly static sense may be a highly interdependent system when the time dimension is introduced. In this sense economics has managed to combine the sophistication of equilibrating forces in an interdependent system with the simplicity of aggregation. Apart from showing how clever economists have been in the past, is this really important?

The main task of the remainder of the book is concerned with analysing this question. To start with, we shall offer a tentative question which will concern us in the next section: what are the implications for aggregation if there exist significant interdependencies in a static context?

ANALYTIC STRUCTURALISM

The second major theoretical perspective identified by Piaget is that of analytic structuralism (1968, pp.8–9, 97–101). Expressed in its simplest form this states that it is the process by which wholes are composed that is primary. The system is no longer the sum of parts, relationships between elements must now also be taken into account. This can be illustrated visually by modifying our original Fig. 2.1 to allow for interdependencies, as in Fig. 2.2

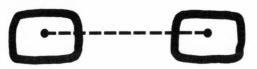

FIGURE 2.2   Inter-relationships

Adding the concept of relation changes entirely the rules of the game as far as system description is concerned. Suppose, for example, we are concerned with the behaviour of chemical compounds. If we have an equal number of atoms of sodium and chlorine, then the resulting complex could be described as an aggregate of the atoms and their rather unpleasant properties as long as there is no reaction between them. However, if each sodium atom reacts with a chlorine atom to form NaCl, then an interesting change takes place in the system. In reacting, sodium loses an electron to a chlorine atom, creating oppositely charged ions of sodium and chlorine, and a bonding relationship results. A poisonous metal and a poisonous gas have combined to create common salt. If we were analysing NaCl using aggregative techniques, adding salt to soup would seem an act of high folly or extreme despair. Similarly, we would expect that H_2O would be easier to breathe than to drink. In this manner aggregation provides a distorting lens through which to view phenomena in cases where relationships between elements are important.

The structuralist perspective as expressed in Fig. 2.2 has been widely applied in most of the social sciences, with economics a notable exception. A chemist studying NaCl would be concerned with the constituent sodium and chlorine ions, *and* the ionic bond between them. Analogously a structuralist in the social sciences builds his models around relationships between component parts. Lévi-Strauss has applied structuralist analysis to anthropological problems with interesting results. In doing so he distinguishes between diachronic analysis, which is concerned with relations in time between elements in a system, and synchronic analysis, which is concerned with relations between elements at a specific point in time. These distinctions are similar to the distinctions between dynamic and static analysis in economics (Hagen, 1961).[5] However they are richer than the economic terms in so far as they imply the existence of *relation* between elements; as we have seen this is not necessarily the case in the use of the corresponding economic terms.

This is a central point that may help to highlight certain aspects of economic analysis; a series of random events over time would be dynamic but not diachronic – there would be no relationship, adjustment process or causality between events. Similarly, a series of independent and unconnected elements at a single point in time would be static but not synchronic – there would be no links or relationships between elements at any given point in time. Now, we can employ dynamic and static perspectives in neoclassical theory, but as we have seen the main type of relationship between elements is expressed in terms of adjustment processes – diachronic relationships. Synchronic relations are conspicuous by their absence. It may be helpful to consider further Lévi-Strauss' structuralist perspective.

In his analysis, Lévi-Strauss uses synchronic relations in a structuralist analysis of kinship systems in primitive societies. He identifies a basic kinship system based on four elements (brother, sister, father, son) and invokes relations between spouses, siblings and parent/child as being important in determining the behaviour of the overall system. These relationships can be expressed in four ways (1) mutuality (attitudes of affection), (2) reciprocity (reciprocal exchanges relationship), (3) rights (a creditor type relationship), (4) obligations (a debtor type relationship) (Lévi-Strauss, 1963, pp.46–9).

Lévi-Strauss interprets his system as *the* basic kinship structure and describes it as 'the true atom of kinship' (1963, p.48). At this point it is worth emphasising that Lévi-Strauss has aroused substantial controversy in the application of his approach; this is technical anthropology and will not concern us here. What is important to us is the form of Lévi-Strauss' approach rather than the content. In this respect his approach contributes a system composed of basic elements and relations expressed in a synchronic or static fashion. The development of his theory is with respect to search for *patterns* in the behaviour of his basic system.

Do approaches like that of Lévi-Strauss have any implications for economics? Interestingly he criticises earlier historical or diachronic approaches to kinship problems as resulting in a chaotic jumble of disconnected explanations of specific behaviour – no pattern is observed synchronically (1963, pp.34–5, 39). The analogous result in economics would be for a specific problem like diversification to be analysed using a multiple regression analysis in which a number of independent variables predominated rather than any underlying belief in a general pattern. Whether this is in fact the case in such studies, we shall leave as an open question for the moment.

We can summarise the structuralist case so far: a system is characterised by relations between its constituent elements; these relations are diachronic (between elements over time) or synchronic (between elements at a point in time) This may be illustrated as in Fig. 2.3. The structure is left open to avoid giving the impression that we are dealing with closed or self contained systems. The system may have relations with other elements or systems both over time and at a point in time. Representations like the above diagram may be implicit

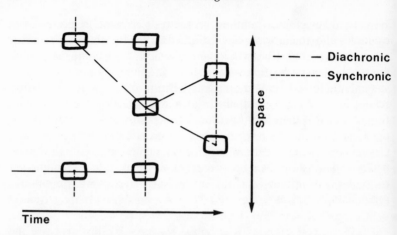

FIGURE 2.3 Synchronic and diachronic relations

in description of complex behaviour as diverse as the formation of salt crystals or growth of kinship systems. The important aspect of this structuralist perspective is that it demonstrates the *complementarity* of synchronic and diachronic relations. Lévi-Strauss emphasises the importance of both types of interdependency (see, for example, 1963, pp. 47 and 89). Analysis of synchronic or diachronic relations in isolation would lead to a distorted view of the system under discussion. They should not be regarded as substitute perspectives.

Seen in this light, the criticisms made by such eminent economists as Arrow and Koopmans of the structuralist perspective seem remarkable for their uncompromising vehemence (see Kay, 1979, pp.210–11). This may appear both puzzling and inconsistent – why should diachronic relations be permissible but not synchronic? One obvious answer lies in the diachronic tradition of economics. Another may be that it is both simple and obvious to associate causality with diachronic relations but not with synchronic relations. This is a point we shall elaborate on in discussing Piaget's third major theoretical foundation – global structuralism.

GLOBAL STRUCTURALISM

So far we have examined briefly two alternative approaches. Aggregation describes complexes as the sum of component elements; analytical structuralism adds the concept of relations between elements as a requisite for adequate system description. A third perspective is provided by those theorists who have interpreted systems as 'emergent totalities' (Piaget, 1968, p.8). Piaget gives as examples the sociologists Comte and Durkheim who conceived of society as an irreducible whole, and the Gestalt psychologists whose approach has been widely (and inaccurately) summarised by the statement, 'the whole is more than the sum of its parts'. The latter school is the most sophisticated global structuralist approach to be found in any of the social sciences. Perhaps the fairest description of the Gestalt approach is provided by translation of the term itself; Gestalt is German for 'form' or 'pattern'. The concern of the Gestalt psychologists has been with the organisation of complexes in their entirety. An example of the holistic nature of Gestalt interpretation is provided in Fig. 2.4.

FIGURE 2.4   Gestalt

If we base consideration of the above complex solely in terms of its constituent elements, then one way of describing the above figure would be as the sum of five plain, white irregular shapes bounded by black lines. This aggregative interpretation would be disputed by analytic structuralists who might argue that aggregation takes no account of the positional relationship of the constituent elements. A third interpretation might be given by a Gestalt psychologist. He would be likely to suggest that the inherent symmetry of the figure would lead to an observer perceiving it as an overlapping triangle and rectangle. Perception of the whole *precedes* perception of the component elements. In this interpretation, rather than state that the whole is more than the sum of parts, as Angyal (1969, p.26) points out it is more accurate to say that aggregation plays no part in whole formation. In the above interpretation, the observer perceives an organised, symmetrical pattern rather than a jumbled aggregate.

There are some important differences between this type of analysis and the other two approaches. While Figs 2.1, 2.2 and 2.3 may be interpreted as models of behaviour, Fig. 2.4 is not a model but a

Gestalt object in its own right. Related to this is the point that the
Gestalt interpretation suggested above is a description rather than an
explanation. Thus the Gestalt perspective is only a first step towards
theory building. However it can provide a basis for such development
(see Kay, 1979, especially Chapter 5).

Within psychology the Gestalt approach may be contrasted with
behaviourism[6] which has also been described as 'stimulus–response
theory' or 'S–R theory'. An action or stimulus elicits a response whose
likelihood of occurrence may be affected by reinforcement (e.g.
reward or punishment). Complex activities are composed of
connected series of S–R units.[7] An example of a behaviourist analysis
of a social situation is provided below; operant refers a class or group
of types of behaviour that produces a common effect on the environment.

Suppose we have a conversation such as the following:
He: What time is it?
She: Twelve o'clock.
He: Thank you
She: Don't mention it.
He: What about lunch?
She: Fine.

Now this conversation can be analysed into separate S–R units. 'He'
makes the *first response*, which is emitted probably to the sight of
'She'. When 'He' emits the operant 'What time is it?', the muscular
activity, of course, produces a sound, which also serves as a
stimulus for 'She'. On the receipt of this stimulus, she emits an
operant herself: 'Twelve o'clock', which in turn produces a stimulus
to 'He'. And so on. The entire conversation may thus be dia-
grammed as:

$$S_I \rightarrow R_A \rightarrow S_A \quad R_C \rightarrow S_C \quad R_E \rightarrow S_E$$
$$\downarrow \quad \nearrow \quad \downarrow \quad \nearrow \quad \searrow$$
$$R_B \rightarrow S_B \quad R_D \rightarrow S_D \quad R_F$$

In such complex activity, then, we can see that what we really have
is a series of S–R connections. The phenomenon of connecting a
series of such S–R units is known as *chaining*, a process that should
be apparent in any complex activity. We might note that there are a
number of sources of reinforcement throughout the chaining
process, in this example the most obvious being the reinforcement

of 'She' by receiving an invitation for lunch and of 'He' by having the invitation accepted. (Calvin (ed.), 1961, pp.377–8)

This extract from a first year psychology textbook was set up as a straw man by Koestler (1967, pp.20–1) to illustrate the limitations of behaviourism and as part of an argument for a structuralist alternative. Koestler's whole book is an excellent well argued repudiation of mechanical atomistic approaches of the type discussed here, whether neoclassical theory in economics or behavioural theory in psychology.

Koestler's argument is recommended in its own right, but here we will concentrate on one aspect of the behavioural approach which should be clear from earlier discussion of Lévi-Strauss' work. This is that the behavioural perspective illustrated above is diachronic. The subject *adjusts* to changes in his environment. There is an explicit causal chain running from left to right in the diagram above. Seen in this light, Gestalt's theory emphasis on structure and organisation as opposed to the diachronic atomism of behaviourism parallels Lévi-Strauss' structural alternative to historical analysis of anthropological problems. However the schism is even more clearcut in this particular psychological debate since Gestalt theory is totally static while behaviourism is dynamic; in anthropology Lévi-Strauss has explicitly recognised the need to synthesise synchronic and diachronic analysis. In fact synchronic analyses similar in form (though of course not content) to Lévi-Strauss' brand of analytical structuralism have been developed and applied in psychology. An important development of this type is Chomsky's approach to psychololinguistics (Chomsky, 1957, 1965) referred to briefly below. While it is useful to contrast Gestalt and behaviourial perspectives for illustrative pruposes, it should be borne in mind that the range of debate in psychology covers the ground of all three of Piaget's theoretical perspectives.

THE STRUCTURALIST APPROACH

In good structuralist fashion we can now attempt to draw together some of the threads of the argument so far. While we have only looked at selected aspects of the structuralist debate in the social sciences, it is hoped that this has been sufficient to demonstrate the main features of a vigorous debate that has developed in psychology, anthropology, linguistics, and sociology.

Even though the symmetry and complementarity of synchronic and diachronic aspects of system description has been argued here, typically it is the latter that has been first to establish territorial claims in the respective disciplines. The intellectual capital invested in diachronic analysis tends to create barriers to the development and application of structuralist analysis.

Visibility of links may be a reason for the generally smoother development of diachronic analysis. Diachronic approaches invoke causal chains as an integral part of their analyses (e.g. neoclassical theory, behaviourism). The association between elements may be clearer and more obvious in a diachronic analysis than in a synchronic analysis. Causality in diachronic analysis helps create this superficial difference which has in many cases proved a simple but misleading basis for theory building.

On the other hand relations between elements in synchronic analysis do not have such distinct roots. In fact the most obvious relations in synchronic analysis may provide a poor basis for theory building. Lévi-Strauss expresses these difficulties:

> What is generally called a 'kinship system' comprises two quite different orders of reality. First, there are terms through which various kinds of family relationship are expressed. But kinship is not expressed solely through nomenclature.... Thus along with what we propose to call the *system of terminology*...there is another system, both psychological and social in nature, which we shall call the *system of attitudes*. (Lévi-Strauss, 1963, p.37)

Since elements in a synchronic kinship system exist simultaneously, causality is no longer a signpost for identification of association between elements. Lévi-Strauss has to emphasise carefully the need to search for the underlying structure of the kinship system. Similarly Chomsky (1965) emphasises the need to identify what he terms 'deep structure' in linguistic analysis. This 'deep structure' is a structural analysis of the semantic relationships between elements of the sentence; analysis of the surface relationship is not adequate. Like Lévi-Strauss, Chomsky feels obliged to emphasise the distinction between surface and underlying structures.

The possibility of such extensive synchronic relations between elements may have significant implications for analysis in economics just as it has had for investigations carried out in the other social sciences.

If the social sciences were a democracy, structuralism would be a major party in the constituencies of each discipline – except economics. The disposition of the economics electorate has been such that in the event of any election, structuralist candidates would surely lose their deposits. This may be because the economics electorate have special problems compared to other regions of the social sciences, or it may reflect a certain Celtic and Anglo-Saxon hardheadedness compared to the suggestible Latin electorates who have been first to vote in significant numbers for structuralist candidates. A more likely explanation favoured here is that the degree of sophistication and level of development of the party machine in economics has both facilitated and necessitated the suppression of parties that were unlikely to be coerced into fellow-traveller status. With this in mind, it is encouraging to see the development of behavioural theory in economics, stimulated first by Simon (1957) and consolidated by Cyert and March (1963). However, the centrality of the concept of satisficing in behavioural theory ensures the approach is essentially diachronic[8] (the decision maker *reacts* to failure to achieve aspiration level; aspiration levels *adjust* to changes in environment) although there are structuralist aspects to Cyert and March's theory (see Kay, 1979, p.90).

The social sciences are not a democracy. What we are concerned with is adequacy of explanation in the respective disciplines. If aggregative techniques are sufficient in this respect in economics, then structuralism is redundant. The question of sufficiency, or otherwise, of aggregation in economics is an essential next step in our argument – before we start putting the case for the prosecution, it is as well to confirm that a crime has been committed. This will be the concern of the next chapter.

One further point may help to summarise the burden of the argument so far. As was pointed out earlier by Loasby, comparative statics in economics has close parallels with the use of thermodynamic equilibrium models in physics. However the theoretical base in thermodynamics is distinctive from that of chemistry. Both are concerned with relations between elements, but thermodynamics is concerned with the forces of *collision* while chemistry is concerned with the forces of *bonding*[9]. The first is dynamic/diachronic, the second is static/synchronic. Both are scientific. If we adopt the one-eyed kinetic view of economic science epitomised by conventional theory we relegate synchronic analysis in economics to the realms of alchemy and mysticism. Chemistry overcame the stigma of a similar dubious standing in the early stages of its development. It is hoped here that structuralist analysis in economics can do likewise.

In the final section here we will focus down from the broad

disciplinary-wide perspective pursued so far, to a specific problem area. The purpose of this is to emphasise some points made earlier, as well as to introduce some new issues that will further help to set the discussion of the next chapter in context. It also helps to provide a bridge with the substantive issues discussed in Kay (1979) as well as introduce Schumpeter's work, an essential part of the later analysis.

THE ACT OF INVENTION

The creative act has been an object of study in psychology, sociology history and economics. As we would expect both diachronic and synchronic analyses of various types have been developed to explain the appearance of novel solutions to problems. There has been much creative thinking about creative thinking. We shall look at Skinner's explanation first.

> The creative mind has never been without its problems, as the classical discussion in Plato's Meno suggests. It was an insoluble problem for stimulus-response psychology because if behaviour were nothing but responses to stimuli, the stimuli might be novel but not the behaviour. Operant conditioning solves the problem more or less as natural selection solved a similar problem in evolutionary theory. As accidental traits, arising from mutations, are selected by their contribution to survival, so accidental variations in behaviour are selected by their reinforcing consequences. . . . The concept of selection is again the key. The mutations in genetic and evolutionary theory are random, and the topographies of response selected by reinforcement are, if not random, at least not necessarily related to the contingencies under which they will be selected. And creative thinking is largely concerned with the production of 'mutations'. (1974, pp.113–14)

Therefore Skinner argues that *reinforcement* explains invention; in this context reinforcement is the reward contingent on the occurrence of the act itself. The reinforcement may be, for example, the inherent beauty of a new symphony or the higher efficiency of a new engine. On the other hand, Hayek advocates a different point of view:

> It is . . . determination of particular actions by various combinations of abstract propensities which makes it possible for a causally determined structure of actions to produce ever new

actions it has never produced before, and therefore to produce altogether new behaviour such as we do not expect from what we usually describe as a mechanism. Even a relatively limited repertory of abstract rules that can be combined into particular actions will be capable of 'creating' an almost infinite variety of particular actions. . . . I know that we[10] both have in this connection been vainly endeavouring to find a really appropriate name for that stratification or layering of the structures involved which we are all tempted to describe as 'hierarchies'. (Hayek, 1978, pp.48–9).

Hayek suggests that creativity is governed by abstract rules operating at the level of unconscious behaviour. Skinner's interpretation is mechanistic, accident-governed and diachronic. Hayek's interpretation is hierarchical, rule governed and synchronic. There exists at any *point in time* a series of hierarchically related rules for creative acts in Hayek's approach.

At first sight we are faced with the (by now) familiar dichotomy between diachronic and synchronic approaches. However, before analysing the two approaches further, we shall consider two other theories of creative acts, this time in a specifically economic context.

The two approaches are those of Schumpeter and Usher, two Harvard economists who were concerned with economic aspects of the inventive process. Although contemporaries and colleagues they developed independent and unrelated interpretations of their area of mutual interest. Schumpeter is especially noted for his concept of 'creative destruction' in which, like Skinner, he draws on biological and Darwinist analogies, in this case to characterise the development of capitalism as an evolutionary process; monopolies innovate, displacing existing products and processes, and providing a continual source of development and renewal in the economy (1954, pp.81–6). The theory is explicitly developed as a dynamic theory in which the growth and decay of firms over time is a direct consequence of innovation. Consequently Schumpeter emphasises technological change as the main engine of capitalist development. In contrast, Usher's approach (1954, 1955) is concerned with the application of Gestalt psychology to problems of invention in which synthesis or 'interweaving' of acts of skill and insight produce novel solutions or inventions. Of course both theories are far richer than this brief sketch credits; however it is sufficient to demonstrate that Schumpeter's approach is diachronic and Usher's is synchronic with its basis in Gestalt psychology.

Of particular interest here is Ruttan's attempt (1959) to demonstrate the *complementarity* of the respective approaches to the problem of technological change. Ruttan argues that Usher's approach augments Schumpeter's and rectifies defects and omissions in the latter's analytical framework. Although Ruttan does not express it in this fashion, he is advocating a marriage of the diachronic and synchronic. Ruttan points out that Schumpeter does not provide an explanation of the inventive process, and indeed similar criticism could be made of Skinner's 'mutation' interpretation of creativity for its ignoring of motivation, pattern and direction in search for solutions. However Ruttan's solution is not to reject the diachronic approach but to integrate it with the synchronic; a similar approach might be feasible for the Skinner/Hayek perspectives. For example, once a Hayek-type rule governed system produces a solution or solution set, a Skinner-type reinforcement process might test solution viability or desirability. The respective approaches may be complements, not substitutes.

A similar argument was used in Kay (1979) in which it was argued that the feedback/adjustment process of satisficing behaviour developed in received Behavioural theory could be used to derive and maintain the Gestalt of managerial preferences for resource allocation developed in that work (pp.95–8); the diachronic supporting the synchronic. Just as reinforcement may be a means to test whether a novel act is useful, so satisficing may be a means to assessing a managerial preference system.

All this helps to emphasise the point made earlier by Lévi-Strauss that a synthesis of the diachronic and the synchronic may be essential for adequate analysis. In the case of Schumpeter's analysis, this is of particular interest here, since it is intended to make use of aspects of Schumpeter's analysis in the context of a broader synchronic perspective in later chapters.

The concept of complementarity between the synchronic and the diachronic will be built upon later. In the next chapter we move from this general contextual standpoint to examine the nature of the firm in economic analysis. In doing so we will establish the building blocks of a structuralist approach to the theory of the firm.

CONCLUSION

This chapter has been concerned with three alternative theoretical approaches as outlined in Piaget's (1968) analysis. The first, that of aggregation, is the general perspective used in economic analysis. Like some related approaches in the other social sciences, such as behaviourism in psychology, neoclassical theory utilises diachronic analysis in its interpretation of the relationship between elements; it then aggregates from a product level base to describe higher level systems.

Diachronic analysis is concerned with the relation between elements over time. It typically involves adjustment processes and causal relations between variables. However, like parallel approaches in the other social sciences, neoclassical theory neglects synchronic relations, or relation between elements at a point in time. Interdependency between elements at a point in time obstructs aggregation and consequently synchronic relations have been largely ignored or neglected in neoclassical theory. By way of contrast, structuralist approaches use such interdependency as the basis for theory building, turning what is a flaw from the point of view of neoclassical theory into a lynchpin of analysis.

By definition, synchronic is static and diachronic is dynamic. However, the reverse does not necessarily apply; a static situation may be characterised by the absence of synchronic relations and similarly dynamic analysis may not throw up diachronic relations. A good example of this is static analysis in neoclassical theory which does not generally recognise synchronic relations, and in so doing facilitates the use of the technique of aggregation.

Piaget identifies two types of structuralist approach, and both are examined above. Analytic structuralism is concerned not only with constituent elements but also the links between them, and theories of this type have been successfully applied in a wide variety of fields such as chemistry, anthropology, psychology and linguistics. Global structuralism is most strongly associated with the Gestalt psychologists and is based on the precept that the whole must be considered as a distinctive entity in its own right.

With the aid of a specific problem area, namely the act of invention, the complementarity of synchronic and diachronic relations was argued above. In the following chapters this theme is developed further, and a framework is built up using both synchronic and diachronic relationships.

3 The Nature of the Firm

In this chapter we shall be concerned with the central problem of the theory of the firm; namely that it does not work. This problem appears less one of poor maintenance or temporary breakdown, more one of fundamentally faulty design. The general malfunctioning of this theory when faced with empirical questions is clearly evident in industrial organisation, the applied field which the theory of the firm should naturally serve. Scherer (1970, p.3) points out that for industrial organisation problems, 'the pure theories of firm and market behaviour have been bogged down on a broad front'. Nelson (1976, p.732) echoes Scherer and points the finger: 'Industrial organisation is in deep intellectual trouble. The source of that trouble is that old textbook theory that we all know so well', while Reekie (1979, p.1) endorses Nelson and complains glumly, 'industrial organisation is a field of intellectual muddle'.

This problem is recognised by theorists. For example, introducing a recent text on the theory of the firm, Crew (1975, p.2) comments; 'neoclassical theory seems to contribute nothing to reconciling the nature of, say, the complex conglomerate on the one hand with the sole trader on the other. Its simplicity, and its assumption of profit assumption, might make it seem closer to the sole trader than the conglomerate. However its ability to provide useful insights into industry, price and even firm behaviour makes it of some relevance to not only small firms but also large complex firms'. The trouble with this rather apologetic apologia is that it does not go nearly far enough in pinpointing the theory of the firms' weaknesses. We shall attempt to put the problem in perspective with the aid of a detailed quote from Hay and Morris:

> Associated with the large size of the companies which have increasingly dominated production are a number of other characteristics. The most significant is diversity of production, which can come about through mergers and acquisition, or through internal diversification. In the US in 1968 the largest 200 firms were

on average operating in 20 different 4-digit industries.[1] 322 were (in 1965) in at least 6 4-digit industries and 12 were in over 40 of them.[2] In 1963, 70 of the largest 100 manufacturing firms were amongst the 4 leaders in 4 or more industries.[3] In the UK in 1958, 60 per cent of manufacturing firms employing over 5,000 were operating in at least 3 industries,[4] and in 1970, of the largest 100 manufacturing firms 94 per cent were to some extent diversified, of which only one-third could be categorized as 'dominant product' diversified firms.[5] Together they account for at least one-third of the output of half the 14 main manufacturing sub-sectors and at least a quarter in 10 of them.[6] In all, approximately 56 per cent of all manufacturing output was produced by firms in at least 2 industries.[7] In addition it must be remembered that even the 4-digit industry classification combines products that may not directly compete being aimed at different segments of a market.[8] (Hay and Morris, 1979, pp.240–1)

The large diversified firm therefore dominates resource allocation in manufacturing industry; in 1970, 33 per cent of US manufacturing net output and 41 per cent of UK manufacturing net output was controlled by the 100 largest firms in the respective countries. Yet this alone does not automatically mean that all is lost for neoclassical theory; if neoclassical theory's base in the single product (or the 'sole trader' as Crew puts it) can be extended into analysis of the large diversified firm without the need for fundamental alteration, then it may need only minor surgical work. Marris defines this problem precisely:

So long as the concept of a 'firm' remained closely associated with the concept of a product, or in the sense that the production possibility set of the individual firm was fixed and exogenous...it mattered little to economic theory whether in practice firms produced only one product or several. A firm's general behaviour would be directly derived from data relating to the products which happened to lie in the production possibility set with which it happened to be endowed: a simple extension of the optimizing rules under single-product monopoly, oligopoly, or for that matter competition, as the case might be, would determine the optimum output of each product and thus, by aggregation, the optimum scale of operations for the firm as a whole. For example, provided all production costs, including managerial and supervisory costs, are truly decomposable among products, this kind of model implies that the general equilibrium allocation of output between all products would not change if, starting from a position of one-firm one-product, some mergers were to occur. (1971, pp.274–5)

By 'decompose' Marris means 'disaggregate'. The problem of decomposability is fundamental in this context. If we can apply neoclassical theory, and aggregate to describe the behaviour of the firm macrosystem, the corollary is that disaggregation is sufficient to provide an adequate description of microsystem product behaviour. It is important to appreciate what decomposability requires. It means that it is a matter of indifference whether Du Pont or Ford produces nylon. The capital market should not raise an eyebrow if Rolls Royce were to take over IBM's latest computer system. Exxon could diversify its refinery output by producing motorbikes as well as petroleum products.

The important point is that decomposability effectively treats the boundaries of firms as arbitrary conventions; the technique presumes that individual products and their associated resources can be shuffled back and forward between firm without any change in expected profitability. This is of course not the case; in general firms exploit market and technological links in their choice of products, for example Du Pont in chemicals, Ford in automobiles, Rolls Royce in engines, IBM. in computers, Exxon in petroleum. Transfer of individual products between those firms should not have a neutral effect on overall profitability.

As far as Crew's remarks above are concerned, the irony is that the exceptional case of diversification to which decomposability conditions are most likely to approximate is that of the conglomerate; if *all* products of the conglomerate are unrelated, then the absence of strong interrelationships means that we can treat each product as an isolated element. Neoclassical theory can be applied at the level of the product and the overall system treated as an aggregate. The sole trader and the conglomerate have far more in common than superficial analysis might suggest. The real challenge to the theory of the firm is posed by the large diversified firm exploiting links between product lines. Consequently, the empirical facts of life as set out by Hay and Morris above, and the theoretical problems of non-decomposability, will be taken to set the context for the discussion of this chapter.

Before we start, however, it is necessary to recognise that non-decomposability is a corollary of structuralism – if we have strong synchronic relations between elements, then we cannot adequately describe the system as the simple sum total of its disaggregated elements. Therefore, what is a hindrance to neoclassical theory and its ability to treat higher level systems as aggregates of lower level systems, is in fact a central feature of structuralist analysis. We shall identify the fundamental source of non-decomposability in firms as being due to *synergy* and employ this concept to build up a structuralist perspective on the firm.

We shall begin by analysing the reasons for the existence of firms as argued by Coase, Alchian and Demsetz, and Williamson. Then we shall extend the analysis to attempt to account for the existence of multiproduct firms.

THE EXISTENCE OF FIRMS

Within the theory of the firm, a great deal of attention has been paid to problems of market structure (in neoclassical theory) and problems of corporate objectives (in managerial and behavioural theories.) However these investigations take for granted an important question which may be simply expressed as; why firms? Although the recent developments in managerial theory do look inside the firm, they tend to be concerned with explanation and prediction of the behaviour of existing corporations, rather than considering how they came to exist in the first place. However the problem of what dictates the formation and form of firms is an important one which has been examined by a number of theorists, notably Coase (1937), Alchian and Demsetz (1972) and Williamson (1975). We shall briefly examine each in turn and then suggest how the analysis may be extended by using concepts based on Ansoff (1965).

Coase asks the question, why are firms necessary? He bases his answer on his interpretation of the price system and the firm as alternative modes of co-ordinating resource allocation. When we move from the market to the firm, the entrepreneur replaces price movements as the director of production. Coase then discusses the conditions under which one co-ordinating device will be preferred to another, and argues that the firm may replace the market when there are costs of using the price mechanism. Coase identifies two major examples of such costs. Firstly, if the firm rather than the market organises co-operative activity between factors of production, then a single employment contract can replace the multiple contracts associated with the price mechanism. Within the limits of the employment contract, firms do away with the need for negotiating a separate contract for each activity performed by factors of production. Secondly, the firm may replace a series of short-term contracts for the supply of a good or service with one entrepreneurial decision or command. While in principle the market could enter into long-term contracts, the difficulties of forecasting may encourage a series of costly short-term contracts instead.

Coase therefore identifies transaction costs as the reason for the existence of firms. While not disagreeing with this rationale, Alchian and Demsetz (1972) extend the analysis by arguing that if factors of production constitute an integrated team in any production process (e.g. two men loading trucks), then marginal productivity cannot be measured and therefore appropriate rewards cannot be easily assessed. Since there is no separable marginal output from the individual factors, there is no obvious basis for allocating rewards to individual factors if the market co-ordinates production. In short, there is a metering problem in terms of production measurement and reward allocation. If, in addition, there is not joint ownership of factors of production there is therefore an incentive for individual factor owners to shirk; the metering problem means the individual factor owner may obtain the benefits of team production as a free rider. However organisation of teams by the firm allows supervision of team behaviour and detailed, continuing observation of individual factor behaviour. Over time the monitor can accumulate and evaluate clues to individual factor contributions[9]. Consequently non-separability of tasks provides a further rationale for the firm in Alchian and Demsetz's view.

Williamson (1975) provides a critical development of both perspectives outlined above. He uses a two-stage analysis to illustrate how hierarchically organised teams may supersede the market mechanism. Firstly, he argues the superiority of unstructured (or peer group) teams over the market under certain circumstances, and secondly he does the same for hierarchically organised teams vis-a-vis peer group teams (peer groups do not differentiate between members in terms of status). We shall discuss both arguments in turn in some detail below since Williamson's work provides a systematic foundation for the examination of the firms versus markets issue.

Williamson's analysis revolves around six core concepts related to transaction costs, (1) *bounded rationality* refers to behaviour that is '*intendedly* rational, but only *limitedly* so' (Simon, 1961, p.xxiv) and derives from human limitations with respect to information processing, (2) *uncertainty/complexity* may mean that it is in principle impossible, or in practice too costly, to obtain all information relevant to a decision. In such circumstances bounded rationality emerges as an important consideration in decision-making; (3) *Opportunism* or deceitful self-interest seeking; (4) *small number* (of involved parties) is a necessary condition for the emergence of opportunism[10] (5) *information impactedness* is usually a consequence of uncertainty and opportunism. It exists when information relevant to a transaction is not equally distributed amongst the parties (6) *atmosphere* results from the circumstances that the exchange relation may not have a neutral effect on the attitudes of participants; the relation itself may provide a direct source of satisfaction or dissatisfaction to participants.

Williamson now argues (pp.41–5) that peer groups may be a more attractive contractual mode than the market if any of three main types of transaction costs obtain. For example, indivisibilities in the utilisation of physical or informational assets may encourage group rather than individual ownership — bounded rationality may impair market contracting (as was already implicitly argued by Coase above), while opportunism may be a cost of using markets in cases of information impactedness. Coase has already indicated how the firm may be superior to the market if bounded rationality holds, and Williamson develops this point further at an earlier point in his work; firstly, unlike market contracts, the decision tree of future decisions does not have to be anticipated in detail, and adaptive behaviour is facilitated, thus economising on bounded rationality. Secondly, repetitious communication in firms facilitates the development of specialised codes (e.g. product descriptions) that further economises on bounded rationality, and are not subject to the same risks of opportunistic exploitation that such codes would be subject to in a market situation. Thirdly, internal organisation co-ordination and direction facilitates convergent expectations as to the future course of future events, and thus helps create compatibility and confidence in decision-making (p.25–6).

Williamson also argues that incentives towards opportunistic behaviour may be reduced by conditions of team ownership arrangements since the individual has sacrificed property rights to the gains accruing from opportunism. This latter point will tend to reduce tendencies towards information impactedness in teams (pp.29–30, 43–4). Further, team membership can insure participants against opportunism by *ex ante* screening and *ex post* monitoring of other participants (pp.43–4). An example of this might be the risks of transactions costs of buying used cars for company use; conducting market transactions with a used car salesman may be risky due to information impactedness and incentives towards opportunism. If the used car salesman is incorporated within the team, his reliability may be gauged by the screening process (and if a satisfactory standard is not achieved he may be rejected) while any remaining opportunistic behaviour may be uncovered and penalised by team monitoring. Even if risks remain due to opportunism or other unanticipated contingencies, team membership acts as insurance by providing income guarantees.

Finally, there may be a gain in 'atmosphere' in teams (pp.44–5). Put simply, some individuals may like to be part of teams. Working together can be a satisfying experience for team members.

While Williamson is more concerned with the distinction between markets and hierarchies as methods of task co-ordination, his analysis of peer group advantages over the market must be set alongside that of Coase, and Alchian and Demsetz as providing an argument for the existence of firms. While Alchian and Demsetz emphasise technological non-separabilities as the main reason for the emergence of firms, Coase emphasises transaction costs, and Williamson developed this latter interpretation by applying the concepts of bounded rationality and opportunism to transactional problems.

THE EVOLUTION OF HIERARCHY

In this section we take the analysis a step further by examining the evolution of hierarchy in teams. In this context, Williamson's comparison of the relative efficiency of peer groups and hierarchies (1975, pp.45–56) provides a valuable basis for discussion.

Williamson argues that unsystematic metering in peer groups leads to possible free-rider abuse, while collective decision-making processes associated with such teams are expensive compared to hierarchical decision-making.

The latter point is illustrated in Fig. 3.1, which illustrates a team with four members. The lines joining the team members indicate possible communication channels. If all members communicate with each other in a collective peer group team, the number of channels required is 6; however if we select one (say A) as a peak co-ordinator who is responsible for communicating with the three other team

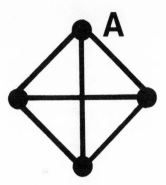

FIGURE 3.1   Team with all channel network

members and making decisions based on these communications, then the number of channels required is reduced to three (see Fig. 3.2). Since we have differentiated status and behaviour of team members, this is now a simple hierarchy.

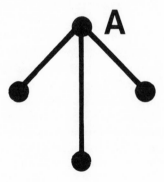

FIGURE 3.2   Team with peak co-ordinator

Maintaining information channels imposes costs, not the least of which is liable to be the time of participants. Williamson suggests that a peak co-ordinator may help reduce these costs, with little or no reduction in the quality of decision making[11]. Since communication costs increase as a function of the square of the number of participants[12] they are liable to be significant for anything other than small teams. Also, differences in bounded rationality between individuals suggests that appointing the most able individual as peak co-ordinator should further improve the quality of decision-making (p.47). Finally opportunism may also encourage the development of hierarchy. Even though peer groups may eliminate some opportunism associated with market transactions, Williamson points out that information impactedness may result in (a) the screening process selecting inferior applicants, (b) a participant leaving the organisation to exploit its trade secrets, (c) shirking (p.47–8). Williamson argues that the peer group is limited in its ability to perform the necessary auditing and experience-rating functions required to control these problems of information-impactedness and opportunism. Appointment of a specialist supervisor permits a systematic approach to the problems of preventing, curbing and/or penalising such abuses. As well as economising on decision-making resources, it also facilitates rapid adaptation to changing circumstances (p.51); by comparison peer group decision-making is costly and time-consuming.

Williamson sets a cost against hierarchies compared to peer groups; there may be a loss in involvement and satisfaction for participants due to the ranking, auditing and rating aspects of hierarchies (p.54–6). A peer group may be preferred due to gain in atmosphere despite possible productivity losses. However, except for small groups, the other costs discussed above will tend to swamp atmosphere considerations. Therefore Williamson's analysis helps demonstrate why the nature of the firm is essentially hierarchical.[13]

However simple hierarchical relations merely serve as the building blocks for the evolution of more complex hierarchies. The problems of bounded rationality may be reduced, not eliminated, by adoption of a simple hierarchical organisation as outlined in Fig. 3.2. Suppose we double the number of team members in this example; the peak co-ordinator now has seven channels to co-ordinate. However the existence of bounded rationality means there is a limit to the number of channels a co-ordinator is capable of administering; he has a finite span of control (pp.126–7). If our co-ordinator in this example is already handling all the channels that he can manage, additional hierarchical levels will have to be added. Fig. 3.3 illustrates one way of developing the team hierarchy.

Bounded rationality therefore leads to finite span of control which in turn creates the necessity for chaining hierarchical levels. However this chaining process leads to progressive loss and distortion in information as it is filtered along a chain from the bottom of the hierarchy to A at the top (pp.126–7). Williamson describes this as a control loss problem resulting from serial reproduction of information. We shall return to this issue later in discussion of organisational form.

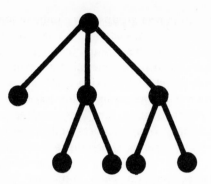

FIGURE 3.3   Complex hierarchy

At this point, however, we shall try to put the preceding discussion into some sort of perspective. What is especially interesting is that transaction costs in general — and bounded rationality in particular — should have taken us so far towards constructing a crude picture of the firm as an administrative unit. Coase's view of the firm did not really conflict with the black box view utilised by neoclassical theory though it did attempt to explain why the black box existed in the first place. On the other hand, Williamson contends that the black box has innards, that these innards are determined by economic factors, and that they in turn are of relevance to economic analysis.

In the next section we shall attempt to carry this analysis one stage further by combining the concept of synergy with that of transaction costs to provide a simple explanation for the existence of the multiproduct firm.

SYNERGY AND TRANSACTION COSTS

Piaget introduces his work on structuralism by bemoaning 'the various meanings it has acquired in the sciences and, unfortunately, at cocktail parties' (1968, p.3). The concept of synergy developed and applied by Ansoff (1965) to the analysis of corporate strategy has succumbed to a similar fate, and no doubt it makes an appearance at the same cocktail parties attended by structuralism. However, rather than demeaning the concepts, this process of trivialisation constitutes an indirect tribute to their power and influence. A simple method of counteracting the process in the case of synergy is to examine what Ansoff meant by the concept.[14]

According to Ansoff, synergy is the 'effect which can produce a combined return on the firm's resources greater than the sum of its parts' (1965, p.75). This has been frequently expressed as $2 + 2 = 5$ since the firms combined performance is greater than the simple aggregate of parts. There is an echo here of the structuralist position as outlined in Chapter 2. We shall take this point up below, but first we shall examine in more detail what is meant by synergy.

Ansoff begins by stating that the firm's characteristics can be regarded as the simple sum of parts if all the products are totally unrelated (p.74). Sales revenue, operating costs and investment funds for the firm as a whole are each obtained by aggregating the values of the respective measure for each component part. Consequently profit is the sum total of profit obtainable from individual parts of the business. However if the component parts are related in some way, synergy may result from joint effects between parts. Ansoff identifies four types of synergy. These are outlined in Table 3.1, together with their possible sources.

TABLE 3.1   Types of synergy

Synergy type	Source
Sales synergy (S)	Common (1) distribution channels, (2) sales administration, (3) advertising, (4) sales promotion or (5) reputation
Operating synergy (O)	Common (1) facilities, (2) personnel, (3) overheads, (4) learning curves or (5) inputs
Investment synergy (I)	Common (1) use of plant, (2) R & D, (3) tooling, (4) raw materials inventories or (5) machinery
Management synergy (M)	Transferability of management experience and skills across parts

SOURCE   Ansoff (1965, pp.75–6).

The crucial aspect as far as each type of synergy is concerned is that it depends on the existence of some common factor between constituent elements (or product markets); for example whether it is a shared consumer (sales synergy), a shared raw material (operating synergy) or shared technology (investment synergy), there is an identifiable link in each case between the elements composing the firm.[15]

We shall define these basic elements in the right-hand column in Table 3.1 as *constituents* and employ them in developing a more micro-analytic interpretation of the firm than is presently provided by neoclassical theory. Transaction cost analysis will be used at this level of analysis.

We can therefore directly associate potential synergy with the degree of relatedness between product/markets administered by the firm measured in terms of the extent to which constituents are shared. We would expect potential synergy to increase with product-market relatedness, *ceteris paribus*. As far as management synergy is concerned, it is derived from the cognitive abilities of managers rather than observable physical links. However, as Ansoff points out (p.76), it too will tend to decline as degree of relatedness declines. This is because management synergy depends on the degree of similarity of management problems between product-markets, and this is turn may be traced back directly to degree of product-market relatedness. Thus, as with other sources of synergy, in the last analysis management synergy is dependent upon the existence of links between product-market areas of the firm.

We can demonstrate the relevance of synergy by considering a simple example. Suppose we have two firms of similar size; one a producer and seller of aluminium tennis racquets, one a producer and seller of aluminium skis. They employ similar technologies and sell to similar consumers. Now suppose one firm was to take over the other or they were to merge; what sort of gains might be possible from the combination of the two product-markets within one firm?

Examples of *sales-synergy* might be sales staff marketing tennis rackets *and* skis to retailers with attendant gains in productivity; further, name or reputation is liable to be transferable *along* shared constituents (e.g. a reputation for quality aluminium goods or sports equipment, or both) and so advertising gains may be realised. *Operating synergy* may be achieved if the similarities in technology permit joint utilisation of plant and equipment, facilitating fuller exploitation of indivisible constituents. *Investment synergy* may be obtained from, say, the expertise of a research team skilled in the development of aluminium skis being made available for the design of aluminium tennis racquets. Finally, *management synergy* may be obtained by spreading scarce managerial skills specific to aluminium sports goods over two product-markets, rather than concentrating them in one limited product-market area.

The list of examples could be extended almost indefinitely. However, those above will suffice to demonstrate how synergy effects may be expressed in economic terms. If we assume that price, cost and output in the ski product-market is held constant, then we can illustrate synergy effects from ski/racquet combination for the racquet product-market with the aid of Fig. 3.4.

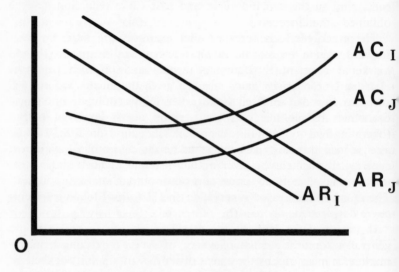

FIGURE 3.4   Synergy effects for one product-market

We will assume that average revenue and average cost for the racquet product-market if it is operated independently is AR_I and AC_I respectively. Now, if it is combined with the ski product-market within one firm and synergy effects exploited, these synergy effects will directly affect the revenue and cost conditions operating in the tennis racquet product-market. If we hold price and output in the ski product-market constant, then the sales synergy effect of reputation transferred through shared constituents depends on the advertising policy after combination. If advertising policy does not change, then the sales synergy effect will be to shift the AR_I curve rightwards, say to AR_J. The sales effect of tennis advertising will be boosted by association with ski advertising; the immediate function of racquet advertising is to promulgate information of/credibility for, this aluminium sports good product, and in this respect it is indirectly assisted by ski advertising/reputation.

Alternatively the firm may take advantage of the advertising boost from skis to reduce direct advertising on racquets to the extent that existing demand is maintained, but at reduced cost for all levels of output; in these circumstances the average cost curve will shift downwards, say, to AC_j and the demand curve does not shift. The actual policy adopted will depend on the marginal relationship between revenue and advertising expenditure, and in practice both some shift in the demand curve and cost curve reduction may be obtained simultaneously.

The synergy effects for the other examples are more straight-forward. Again we assume that price, cost and output in the ski market are constant. If we combine racquets and skis, then, firstly the sales staff productivity gains means a given output of racquets will cost less to make and sell (sales synergy); secondly, technological economies reduce this cost contribution at all levels of output (operating synergy); and thirdly productivity gains from R & D should also reduce this cost element at all levels of output (investment synergy). In each case, a given output of tennis racquets should cost less to make, holding price cost and output of skis constant. Therefore, in each case the synergy effect is to shift the average cost curve downwards, say to AC_j.

If we allow the level of operations in skis to vary, we would generally expect the strength of synergy effect for the racquet product-market (as measured by the extent of the downward shift of the cost curve) to be directly related to the level of ski operations. If skis are a minor activity of the firm in comparison to tennis racquets, we would expect its synergy potential to be limited as far as tennis racquets is concerned. We would typically expect the strength of the synergy effect for tennis racquets to increase as ski-ing activity increases.

We have omitted the example of management synergy from detailed discussion; this is because the effect of management synergy depends on the specific application of management resources. Depending on the particular problem tackled by management, management synergy effects may be to shift demand or cost curves – or both.

Therefore examination of sources of synergy gains in our simple example has helped to illustrate two types of synergy effects, the first being a shift rightwards of the demand curve, the second being a downwards shift of the average cost curve, in both cases measured against constant operating characteristics in the other product-market. This point merits emphasis, since interpretation of synergy as a form of economy of scale is common in the literature[16]. However it is a distinctive concept; synergy effects involve *shifts* in the cost and revenue functions, not movements *along* the cost curve as implied by economies of scale.

Why then have the two concepts been so frequently fused (or confused) in the past? The reason is that economies of scale may be regarded as joint effects of perfectly related activities; they are derived from the same sharing of constituents that generates synergy in Table 3.1, but in this case we are dealing with the special case of perfect or complete sharing of constituents; the joint effect resulting from the combination of two identical activities is recorded as a downward movement along the cost curve (economies of scale) rather than a shift in the cost curve (synergy effect). Therefore economies of scale may be regarded as applying to the *limiting case* of activity relatedness in which all constituents are identical.

For this reason we shall not talk in terms of economies of scale in subsequent analysis, since they should be rightly regarded as being associated with a special case in which management maximise synergy. The synergy gains from maximum activity relatedness are interpretable as economies of scale and as downward movements along a cost curve, not shifts in cost curves.

At the other extreme of activity relatedness, we might naturally expect synergy to be zero when activity relatedness is zero. However, Ansoff (1965, p.76) suggests, 'if . . . the problems in the acquired area are new and unfamiliar, not only will positive synergy be low, but there is a distinct danger of a negative effect of top-management decisions'. Thus, low activity relatedness may be associated with negative synergy.[17] Thus, absence of links does not necessarily have a neutral effect on combination. Managerial experience can be an inhibiting as well as a facilitating factor.

However there is an implicit assumption in our argument up to this point, that combination by merger, take-over, or internal development is required to exploit synergy benefits. This is not necessarily the case since *all* the examples of synergy benefits discussed earlier may be tradable in the market place. The tennis racquet firm may obtain sales synergy by paying commission on the sale of racquets by the ski firm sales force[18]; it may obtain operating synergy by synchronising reciprocal leasing of factory space and machines with the ski firm; it may obtain investment synergy by contracting the ski R & D team to do extra-mural research on aluminium tennis racquets; and it may obtain management synergy by employing ski management on a consultancy basis. Therefore, in general synergy gains from combination may also be exploited by market transactions, although the precise distribution of these gains will depend on the outcome of bargaining between participants.

Why then should combination by merger or take-over be necessary to achieve synergy gains? The answer is transaction costs, in particular costs associated with bounded rationality and opportunism. First of all, as Coase pointed out, difficulties of forecasting (a consequence of bounded rationality in Williamson's analysis) may favour short-term rather than long-term contracts in the market place. In the face of short-term contracts the firm may be particularly vulnerable to transaction costs resulting from opportunism and bounded rationality. For example the ski-firm may introduce a new ski and instruct their sales force to concentrate all their energies on marketing the ski; in such circumstances the sales outlet for tennis racquets may be choked off completely. Also, the ski-firm may start selling in an overseas market that takes up plant and equipment required by tennis racquets; reciprocal leasing agreements for operating synergy may not be renewed if ski plant and machinery have no spare capacity.

In both these cases the ski-firm may act opportunistically – e.g. they may claim to the tennis racquet firm they are instructing their sales force to market the tennis racquets, while instructing their sales force otherwise; and when the leasing option is taken up by the tennis-racquet firm, things may 'go wrong' – lack of co-operation, 'accidents' mis-scheduling of men and facilities supplied by the ski firm etc. may force the racquet firm to cancel the leasing agreement. Bounded rationality and information impactedness in both these examples means that the racquet firm is vulnerable to opportunism. However, in the face of short-term contracts, opportunism may not even be necessary – the short-term contract may simply be allowed to lapse and not be renewed.

As far as market trading of the other two examples of synergy are concerned, information impactedness is also liable to be of relevance both from the point of view of supply of R & D services and management consultancy, information impactedness creates the pig-in-a-poke type problem discussed earlier in the context of the used car salesman example. Bounded rationality and opportunism again result in transaction costs.

There is a further point worth emphasising here in the context of a small numbers bargaining problem. As mentioned earlier, the distribution of synergy gains traded in the market place depends on the outcome of bargaining between participants. Suppose our tennis racquet firm has been spectacularly successful in capturing most of the gains from synergy in its negotiations with the ski firm. This would be reflected in substantial rightward shifts of the average cost curve in

Fig. 3.4. This would result in significant increases in potential profitability for the racquet firm. However the corresponding demand and cost functions for the ski firm would only register slight shifts by comparison with the racquet firm, with similar implications for the profitability gains from synergy for that firm. In such circumstances there are liable to be strong pressures towards opportunistic behaviour on the part of the poor relation, and/or moves to internalise the synergy benefits by internal developments, take-over or merger. For example, our ski-firm has little to lose by abandoning the contract with the tennis firm and/or acting opportunistically, but it stands to gain a great deal if it can somehow appropriate the synergy gains presently enjoyed by the racquet firm. One obvious way of doing this would be by starting an aluminium tennis racquet division of its own, whether by starting from scratch or via merger/take-over.

In short, the *higher* the relative share of synergy gains appropriated by a firm through market transactions, in general the more vulnerable it is to short-term opportunism or withdrawal. On the other hand, the *lower* the relative share of synergy gains appropriated by the firm the more advantageous the firm itself is liable to find opportunism or withdrawal. Therefore market agreements to trade synergy may well turn out to be highly unstable for most cases even if feasible in principle. In such cases the abandonment of the contract, and possible incorporation of synergy within the firm, are likely.

In this section we have discussed how synergy and transaction costs can provide a rationale for the multi-product firm. In the next section we shall build on this argument in a first approach to the question of the composition of specific multi-product firms.

SYNERGY MAPS

Suppose we make the generous assumption that all types of synergy identified in Table 3.1 are fully exploitable in the tennis racquet/ski example. Bearing in mind that all synergy is derivable from joint effects or links between product-markets, we can illustrate this diagrammatically in Fig. 3.5.

A similar concept is illustrated in Child (1977) in which activities are grouped by related clusters. Child's analysis is a helpful approach derived from organisation theory in which the logic of grouping by related areas is demonstrated. The analysis here develops this idea further and introduces new aspects such as the role of transaction costs and environmental technoloqical change.

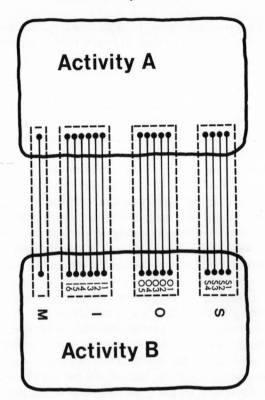

FIGURE 3.5(a)   Specific synergy links

S = Sales Synergy
O = Operating Synergy
I = Investment Synergy
M = Management Synergy

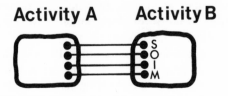

FIGURE 3.5(b)   General synergy links

We shall use the term activity to describe a specific product market; in Fig. 3.5 we may take activity A to be tennis racquet, activity B to be skis. Fig. 3.5(a) identifies all possible synergy links according to their enumeration in Table 3.1: for example 04 is operating synergy resulting from common learning curves, while 14 is investment synergy resulting from common raw materials inventories. If we can treat the components of each of the four main types of synergy as exploitable as a group, then we can amalgamate components into their major categories as in Fig. 3.5 (b).

In practice, only some of the specific synergy types may be exploitable; for example, for sales synergy there may be advertising links but completely separate distribution channels. Further, specific synergy types may be only partially exploitable; for example common inventories may be feasible for some raw materials, but not for others. Obviously joint effect on profitability is directly related to the extent that joint effects can be exploited for synergy gain.

However, we have assumed that all potential joint effects are obtainable in the tennis racquet/ski example; what are the implications for firm versus market co-ordination of exploitation of synergy? Quite simply, the transaction costs associated with market organisation are liable to be prohibitively high compared to firm organisation of the system. From Coase's analysis, we would expect that market trading of synergy gains would require a series of complex and detailed contracts forged at the level of specific synergy links, or at even lower levels. Williamson's analysis can also be applied at the level of specific synergy links to identify transactions costs resulting from bounded rationality and opportunism in market transactions for each link. Therefore, a cat's cradle of expensive bilateral contracts can be substituted by simple entrepreneurial co-ordination and direction if firm rather than market co-ordination is adopted. A further point is that the potential for instability in a market system of synergy trading (discussed at the end of the last section) is liable to be directly related to the number of synergy links; since potential profitability will increase with the number of synergy links, *ceteris paribus*, so do the corresponding rewards for opportunism or unilateral withdrawal.

In short, the greater the number of effective synergy links between two activities the greater is resultant profitability. Further, market co-ordination is likely to become both more expensive and potentially unstable relative to firm co-ordination as the number of effective synergy links increases. *Ceteris paribus*, we would expect firms to attempt to maximise the number of synergy links between their

activities because of profitability considerations, and to do this by
incorporation within the firm, rather than through market transaction. Yet this simplistic conclusion is obviously open to immediate
challenge and refutation; while a large number of firms operate with a
high degree of relatedness between activities (e.g. in food, drink,
tobacco, petroleum industries in most countries), many others have
only loose or minimal links, as in the case of the giant conglomerates.
Obviously our analysis of transaction costs and synergy links so far
has provided us with, at best, an incomplete description of the
rationale for the multiproduct firm.

We can illustrate this problem by developing synergy maps as a tool
of analysis. We shall use the general synergy links as described in Fig.
3.5(b) for simplicity, with three modifications; firstly, we shall
represent the relative size of the activity (say in terms of value added)
by the extent of the bounded area for the activity in the diagram;
secondly, we shall assume that management synergy will in practice be
operationalised in the form of sales, operating or investment synergy
and will therefore be amalgamated within the respective categories
where appropriate; thirdly, the importance of synergy links in terms
of their effect on profitability will be represented by the thickness of
the link between activities. Three examples of the use of synergy maps
are given in Fig. 3.6.

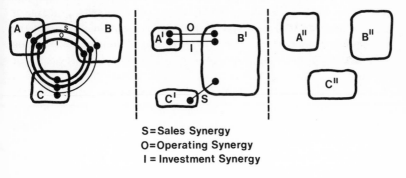

S = Sales Synergy
O = Operating Synergy
I = Investment Synergy

Fig. 3.6(a)   Firm Alpha   Fig. 3.6(b)   Firm Beta   Fig. 3.6(c)   Firm Omega

FIGURE 3.6   Synergy maps

Firm Alpha is a development of the familiar racquet/ski example.
Product market *A* is aluminium tennis racquet, product market *B* is
aluminium skis, while product market *C* is aluminium fittings for

sailing dinghies, and has been created by subsequent diversification. Measured in terms of resources used, C is not as important as A and B; also while strong technological links with A and B provide substantial synergy benefits, sales synergy is weak, as indicated by the thinness of the link, possibly because sailing customers of Alpha are dinghy manufacturers rather than final consumers as in A and B. Image as a manufacturer of aluminium sports goods may be a residual source of synergy for Alpha.

Firm Beta is a competitor of Alpha in aluminium skis, B' being the ski division in this case. Division A' is aluminium kitchen ware and B' is ski-wear. Now, Beta has obviously followed a distinctive line of development compared to Alpha. Alpha may be described as a manufacturer of aluminium sports goods, but Beta has no such continuous links, It has exploited its technological base in aluminium skis by diversifying into aluminium kitchen ware; distribution channels and marketing procedures for A' and B' and dissimilar and consequently sales synergy is effectively non-existent. However, Beta has exploited its ski-ing image and distribution channels by diversifying into ski-wear, although the method of design and production in C' has no effective technological links with B'. It is worth noting that while all activities exploit synergy links of some kind, there are no direct links between A' and C'.

Omega's three activities are electronic calculators (A''), aluminium skis (B'') and glass products (C''). Although it might be possible to squeeze some little synergy out of this combination, we have assumed synergy is non-existent due to absence of relatedness between activities. Omega is therefore a genuine conglomerate in its operation of unrelated activities.

If it were the case that Alpha, Beta and Omega were the only three firms operating in the aluminium ski industry, then Fig. 3.6 can also provide a perspective on competition in this industry. In terms of our size measure, Beta is the largest competitor in the market, B' being substantially larger than B and B''. While Beta partially exploits competences developed in B' in its A' and C' divisions, its competitors have very different backgrounds; Alpha competes as an all-round aluminium sports good manufacturer while Omega's division B'' has no links with other activities to complement its involvement in the aluminium ski industry.

In fact, industrial competition is characterised in general by a heterogenous mix of corporate types of which the above is only one example. For example, in 1969–70 firms competing in the UK soft drinks industries included Allied Breweries, Cadbury/Schweppes, and Reckitt & Coleman. Allied Breweries manufactured and marketed alcoholic and soft drinks; Cadbury/Schweppes manufactured and marketed confectionery, cakes, preserves, canned foods and convenience foods as well as soft drinks; while Reckitt and Coleman manufactured and marketed a wide variety of goods in addition to soft drinks, including pharmaceuticals, mustard, shoe polish and disinfectants (Channon, 1973, pp.55, 63). While accurate synergy maps would require detailed investigation of each firm, we would expect that Allied Breweries synergy map would display rich interconnections in a similar manner to firm Alpha. Correspondingly, we would expect Cadbury/Schweppes' varied mix of markets and technologies within food and drink to lead to a synergy map bearing a strong family resemblance to firm Beta, while the context in which Reckitt and Coleman's soft drink ventures are set is similar to that of the divisional operations of the unrelated firm, Omega.

Therefore, mapping synergy not only creates a portrait of the multi-product firm, it also helps correct the narrow picture of industrial competition as taking place in isolated markets. While this latter point is not a question we shall pursue further here, it is worth emphasising that Alpha, Beta and Omega (and Allied Breweries, Cadbury/Schweppes, Reckitt and Coleman) are liable to have different perspectives (and strengths/weaknesses) with respect to competition in the markets they share as a consequence of the different strategies they have adopted. Our concern will continue to be focused on the firm rather than the industry. In the next section we shall discuss how the view of the firm developed here relates to existing interpretations. In doing so we shall make a distinction between strategic and tactical issues in the firm.

THEORIES OF STRATEGY AND TACTICS

The type of of problems we have been exploring in this chapter would be termed strategic by Ansoff; 'strategic decisions are primarily concerned with external, rather than internal, problems of the firm and specifically with selection of the product-mix which the firm will produce and the markets to which it will sell' (1965, p.18). However while the latter part of this definition describes the problem area we have been concerned with, the first part appears to confuse the issue. Ansoff interprets strategic to mean 'pertaining to the relation between the firm and its environment' (p.18), while operating decisions include such problems as pricing (p.8); yet pricing decisions in oligopoly surely depend on firm/environment relations, while synergy considerations largely revolve around *internal* relationships between activities. The two parts of the definition are not mutually consistent.

We can resolve this ambiguity quite simply. Just as it helped to refer back to the original authority (Ansoff) for clarification in the case of synergy, so it may help to look for guidance to original authority,[19] in the case of strategy; this is provided by substituting 'business' for 'war', 'competition' for 'fighting', 'product-market' for 'combat', in the following quote.

> The conduct of War is, therefore, the formation and conduct of the fighting. If this fighting was a single act, there would be no necessity for any further subdivision, but the fight is composed of a greater or less number of single acts, complete in themselves, which we call combats. . . . From this arises the totally different activities, that of the *formation* and *conduct* of these single combats in themselves, and the *combination* of them with one another, with a view to the ultimate object of the War. The first is called *tactics*, the other *strategy*. (Clausewitz, 1968, p.172)

This interpretation is from the nineteenth-century military strategist Carl von Clausewitz, and neatly expresses the essential difference between the approach developed above, and standard theory of the firm. The 'formation and conduct' of single product-market or activities is the concern of neoclassical theory and, on the applied side, the structure-conduct-performance approach in industrial organisation. These perspectives are *tactical* in being concerned with individual markets taken one at a time. Since we are concerned with the problem of combinations of activities within the firm, our approach is *strategic*. The difference can be illustrated in Fig. 3.6. Firstly, firm Beta may have to make a decision about pricing and output decisions for division B' competing against B and B'' in the aluminium ski industry *given* synergy links and the level of activity in other divisions; this is a tactical decision. Secondly, firm Beta may make decisions concerning whether or not A', B' and C' are the appropriate combination of activities to operate *given* cost and revenue conditions for the respective activities; this is a strategic decision. The firm has to make both tactical and strategic decisions in

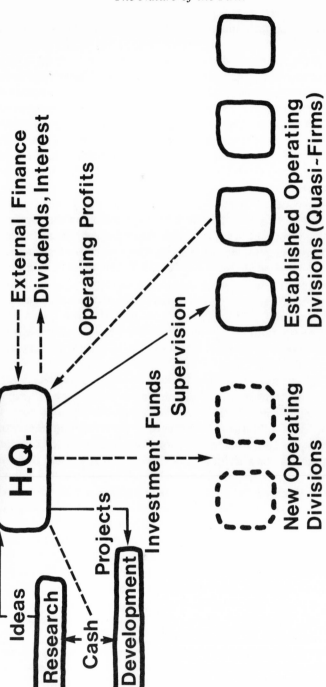

SOURCE   Marris, 1971, p.280.

FIGURE 3.7   A transcendent M-form corporation

allocating resources and while the two types of decision are complementary, they are distinctive. Seen in this light, the received theory of the firm reduces to the theory of the activity; it is not surprising that it has had difficulty in dealing with the firm *per se*, since in this arena it is a theory of tactics applied to fundamentally strategic questions.

We can further demonstrate where this synergy based approach fits in by considering Marris' solution to non-decomposability. After stating the problems associated with decomposability (discussed at the start of this chapter), Marris confirms that the firm cannot be easily decomposed, and that there are, 'almost always' common elements between activities in terms of management skills likely to affect choice of activity (1971, p.275). Marris bases his solution on the concept of the transcendent multi-divisional corporation illustrated in Fig. 3.7.

The transcendent corporation is one which perceives that there may exist, or be created, opportunities for actively changing their environment. These possibilities are generated by R & D or other growth opportunity creating activities of development, such as market analysis. (Marris, 1971, pp.274–80). Marris also identifies an 'immanent' corporation type, which is one in which the growth opportunity creating development box is missing; it does not actively pursue new opportunities.

For our purposes here, the important aspect of Marris' distinction between transcendent and immanent is the base it provides for his signposting of recommended theoretical development. He recommends a split theory of the firm in which one part would investigate the behaviour of divisions or quasi-firms (in our terms product-markets or activities) *as if the firm was immanent* (it may be immanent or transcendent in practice). Removing the development link permits analysis of activities one at a time using an extension of oligopoly (pp.282–3). The firms operating profits is the aggregate of reported operating profits of individual activities (p.282).

The second part of this theory would analyse the growth/operating relationship as presented and decided at the level of the corporation *as a whole*. The optimal growth rate for the corporation is expressed as a function of operating profit. Relevant variables such as growth and dividends are derived at the level of the firm rather than the activity (with operating profit an exceptional variable in being derived from, and decomposable to, activity level).

Marris' split theory is a theory of atomistic association (aggregation) on the one hand, and a theory of emergent totalities (global structuralism) on the other. But according to Piaget; 'over and beyond the schemes of atomist association on the one hand and emergent totalities on the other, there is however, a third (which) adopts a relational perspective, according to which it is neither the elements nor a whole that comes about in a manner one knows not how, but the relations among elements that count' (1968, p.8). This third perspective is that of analytic structuralism discussed in Chapter 2, and indeed it should be obvious from the analysis of that chapter that a synchronic approach to resource allocation in the firm has been pursued here. Synergy is by definition synchronic in its linking of activities.

Instead of regarding non-decomposability as a problem hindering model building, this chapter has been concerned with exploring the possibility of explicitly incorporating a major source of non-decomposability (synergy) into theoretical analysis. The view is taken here that Marris specified well the nature of the theoretical issues posed for the theory of the firm, but that his solution is unsatisfactory particularly with regard to retention of aggregation as a method of higher level description. It is disappointing that having diagnosed the ailment, an inappropriate cure was prescribed. Similarly Williamson (1975) discusses the evolution of hierarchy to cope with the problems of the multiproduct firm; however he does not utilise transaction cost analysis in a general approach to multiproduct combination despite the fact that his framework is ideally suited for this purpose.[20]

In short, synergy is synchronic and a fundamentally structuralist concept identifying relations between elements. It is an embarrassment to neoclassical theory which typically treats such relations as an obstacle to rigorous analysis; for example, if synergy is expressed in the form of shared overheads, the overheads may be ignored or arbitrarily allocated to individual product markets. In this fashion, decomposability is apparently imposed on the system at the expense of distorting perception of the underlying nature of the system and its behaviour. It is strongly argued here that rather than attempting to decompose the system, the synchronic relations expressed in the form of synergy should be developed in a more appropriate structuralist theoretical framework.

In the next chapter we shall further develop the synchronic interpretation of the firm argued here, and augment our analysis by introducing diachronic features into the theory. In doing so we hope to begin to make some progress towards explaining differences in the strategies of firms.

CONCLUSION

This chapter has examined the nature of firms — why they exist and how they operate and conduct their business. The central concern has been with the concept of synergy and in fact this is a fundamentally structuralist idea since it indicates the *links* between product markets. As Marris points out, neoclassical theory has typically treated the firm as an amalgam of independent product markets; synergy links contradict this vision of a decomposable economy.

As a casual experiment in contrasting the perspective of neoclassical theory and the approach developed here, it is interesting to compare how the respective approaches would analyse the firms Alpha, Beta and Omega in Fig. 3.6. Neoclassical analysis would have little difficulty in dealing with the decomposable conglomerate Omega, but the relatively synergy-rich Alpha and Beta are more troublesome cases. A neoclassical analysis would attempt to disaggregate the respective systems either by ignoring the synergy links between product markets, or by arbitrary allocation of shared functions for costs to individual products. The approach developed here differs from neoclassical theory in that the synergy links are retained as an integral part of the analysis. The analysis does not attempt to break the firm down into constituent products any more than chemistry attempts to analyse molecules as aggregates of constituent atoms – and for similar reasons. The synchronic relations indicated by the synergy links contribute to a structuralist perspective of resource allocation problems.

A further difference with respect to neoclassical theory is the emphasis on bounded rationality. Whereas neoclassical theory is built on perfect knowledge, consideration of bounded rationality in this chapter demonstrates not only the reasons underlying the evolution of hierarchy, but also the source of transaction costs that leads to firm co-ordination of synergy as opposed to market trading.

4 Technological Change and Internal Organisation

In this chapter our main purpose is the further development and refinement of synergy maps as an analytical tool. We shall be particularly concerned with the relationship between synergy and internal organisation and also the effect of environmental technological change on corporate strategy.

To start with, however, we shall be concerned with an issue that relates to a previous work (Kay, 1979). The problem we shall be concerned with in this section is the relationship of this preceding analysis to the present work. In a sense this represents a short detour or diversion from our main concern with developing synergy maps, but it is useful to see how our current approach relates to that adopted in the previous work. After this sidestep we shall return to the task of developing synergy maps and examining their implications. Underlying this latter part of the chapter is the argument that transaction costs result in multiproduct operation. We have strongly argued the importance of transaction costs in the previous section on the multiproduct firm. So far synchronic relations have been analysed and techniques for devising synergy maps discussed. However as might be expected from the discussion of Chapter 2, this analysis is incomplete. Diachronic relations are absent so far, and a central purpose of this chapter is to rectify this omission.

However the first concern here will be the interpretation of the previous work (Kay, 1979) into the present argument. The previous work utilised a hierarchical open systems framework which is easily accommodated within a structuralist perspective; in fact it was developed as a general systems theory following the work of L. Von Bertalanffy, a theoretician in biology cited by Piaget as the first to introduce an explicitly structuralist approach in that discipline (1968, p.46–7). Thus, both the previous and present analyses are to be seen as following in the same structuralist tradition; however as we shall see, there are also important differences in the respective interpretations.

We shall start by looking at the internal development of change (or innovation) as argued in Kay (1979). The hierarchical framework of resource allocation introduced there is related to the transcendent corporation form of Marris. In this fashion we relate resource allocation considerations to internal organisation at peak co-ordinator level, and then we proceed to do the same at activity level; synergy maps describing corporate strategy for combination of activities are related to internal organisation form.

Having started with consideration of change endogenous to the corporation, we conclude with exogenous change. The effects of change in the environment on corporate strategy is discussed, and a rationale provided for differences in combination of activites between firms. Diachronic relations inside and outside the firm are therefore a prime concern of this chapter. However, we begin by looking at 'the innovating firm'.

THE INNOVATING FIRM

In Kay (1979) a theoretical approach to resource allocation for innovation in the firm was developed. Then, as now, a major concern of the work was the distorting effect that aggregation has in describing behaviour at the level of the firm. Here we shall briefly summarise the earlier argument and suggest how it may be integrated with the present analysis.

The starting point of the earlier work was that when research and development (R & D) is analysed at project level, these projects typically have a high degree of associated uncertainty (Chapter 2, pp.9–29). This is an unavoidable fact of life with innovation; since such projects are by definition unique,[1] existing knowledge and experience is of only limited use in cost and revenue prediction for the final output, whether it is a new product or new process. Faced with intractable uncertainty, project-based approaches such as neoclassical theory break down; even approaches explicitly developed to deal with uncertainty such as that of Arrow (1962, 1971(a)) do not provide satisfactory representations of the R & D process (Kay, 1979, pp.30–40).

Yet, when analysed at corporate level, the characteristics of resource allocation to R & D appear rather different. Empirical evidence suggests that management appear to seek a balance between innovating and operating resources in the large modern corporation, and that managerial resource preferences tend to be fairly well-defined and stable; for example R & D is generally allocated annually on a percentage of sales basis (Kay, 1979, pp.58–84). Further, allocation to the R & D budget tends to precede selection of projects in the large corporation; if some project based technique was used to determine overall allocations to R & D versus other resources uses, the R & D budget would be decided simultaneously with the selection of projects.

These considerations encouraged the development of a framework for corporate resource allocation based on the idea of firm as a hierarchically organised system (Kay, 1979). This system has a relatively stable set of managerial preferences for resource allocation; resources are distributed in a 'top down' fashion, rather than in the 'bottom up' fashion of aggregative project-based perspectives. A suggested hierarchical system is illustrated in Fig. 4.1.

In Fig. 4.1, an overall allocation is decided between resources for innovation adoption/generation and resources for operations (production/marketing) in quadrant 1. The amount allocated to innovation as a whole in quadrant 1 acts as a constraint on distribution to component resource uses in quadrant 2. The amount allocated to innovation generation (R & D) constrains the amount allocated to development and research in quadrant 3, while the latter allocation acts as a constraint for the split between basic and applied research in quadrant 4. In each case, allocation is decided on the basis of a set of indifference curves outlining managerial preferences for resource combinations in the respective constrained choices. Utility for each combination is derived from the contribution each bundle of resources makes to survival potential of the firm in the long run. Because of competitive pressure, no other goals deflect choice away from that allocation that maximises survival potential[2].

While neoclassical theory is based on aggregation of product/project level analysis, the approach outlined above is based on Gestalt perception and organisation of managerial preferences for resources.[3] As such, higher level systems are perceived as wholes in the approach above, not as the aggregates of lower level systems. In Piaget's terms this is obviously a global structuralist approach to problems of resource allocation in the firm, and interestingly there is a close relationship between the resource allocation decision expressed in quadrant 1, and Marris' Transcendent Corporation as illustrated in Fig. 3.7. As well as providing the organisational basis of Marris' global structuralist growth theory, the relationship between operating and growth (research/development) in Fig. 3.7 may be regarded as the

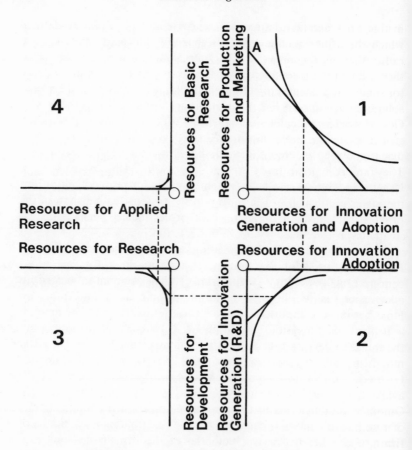

FIGURE 4.1   Hierarchical structure of resource allocation

institutional parallel of quadrant 1; headquarters management in Fig.
3.7 decide allocations between operating and research/development.[4]

However, the management resource preference system as outlined
in Fig. 4.1 is not plucked out of thin air; it is argued (pp. 95–8) that
negative feedback[5] generally provides the mechanism for derivation
and maintenance of this system. The appropriate 'Gestalt' is built up
through interaction between firm and environment, past resource
allocations providing information on which to base revised resource
preferences. In this connection it is argued that the concept of
satisficing in behavioural theory provided the necessary negative
feedback mechanism (p.97).

It is strongly emphasised (p.97) that behavioural theory is regarded in this work as potentially *complementary* to optimising theory (of which the utility maximising approach developed was an example) rather than as a competing theoretical approach. Thus, optimising theory might model steady state allocations, while behavioural theory (or similar approaches) might model the process of attainment of that solution. Seen in terms of the distinctions outlined in Chapter 2, the Gestalt system of managerial preferences is concerned with static structures, while behavioural theory is concerned with dynamic/diachronic relations involved in building up these static structures. They are complementary, in the same spirit Ruttan argued that Usher's and Schumpeter's approaches are complementary, and after the manner in which it was suggested Skinner's behaviourism could provide mechanisms for deriving and testing Hayek's rule-governed creativity process.

Consequently the hierarchical system of managerial preferences in Fig. 4.1 is fashioned and designed by diachronic forces.[6] Yet the concern of analysis in the present work is the determinants of resource allocation to activities, rather than innovation generation/adoption. How does this fit into the earlier framework?

It is assumed here that allocations to activities are constrained by the choice represented in quadrant 1 in Fig. 4.1. The diagram has been modified slightly to indicate the amount allocated to activities; this is OA in quadrant 1. For any particular time period, OA is the amount available for operations; for example if our firm was Alpha, Beta or Omega respectively in Fig. 3.6, OA would represent the total amount of resources available for distribution to the three divisions of each firm.[7]

Thus, synergy maps can be integrated within the hierarchical framework developed earlier. In the next section we shall further discuss the question raised here in connection with the Transcendent Corporation; that is, the relationship between resource allocation and internal organisation.

INTERNAL ORGANISATION AND SYNERGY MAPS

The last chapter was concerned with the implications of transaction costs for the theory of the firm. It was argued that the large multiproduct or diversified firm was the central phenomenon requiring analysis and explanation by this theory, and it was suggested that transaction costs could provide useful insights to this problem. In

a sense, analysis has proceeded in two direction at this point; in one
direction, Williamson has investigated the form of internal
organisation adopted by the multiproduct firm (1975, pp.132–54),
while the concern of the last chapter was with the synergy basis of
activities in the multiproduct firm. Since analysis of internal
organisation and synergy maps in the last chapter have common roots
in transaction cost analysis, it may be possible to relate synergy maps
to internal organisation. That is the purpose of this section, and we
shall begin by summarising Williamson's approach to internal
organisation.

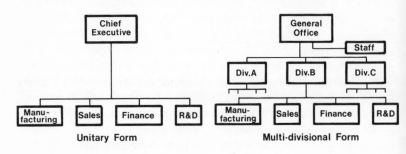

FIGURE 4.2   Organisational form

In charting the evolution of organisational form, Williamson builds
on Chandler's (1966) analysis of the historical development of the
corporation. Chandler associates the late nineteenth century with the
widespread appearance of the large, single product, multifunction
corporation in the US. This function based corporate structure
(unitary form or 'U-form' in Fig. 4.2) permitted efficient specialisa-
tion/division of labour and attainment of economies of scale
(Williamson, 1975, pp.133).

However, expansion of the U-form corporation eventually leads to
an intolerable level of strain on this particular organisational form.
Firstly, information transmission and processing becomes increasingly
inefficient. Since interfunctional co-ordination for each product line is
still carried out at chief executive level, a bottleneck is created at this
level (Williamson, 1975, pp.133–4). Bounded rationality considerations creates finite span of control, and mean that expansion of
the firm requires additional hierarchical levels; the 'chaining' or
serial reproduction of information leads to progressive loss and
distortion of information transmitted up through successive layers in
the organisation and results in the 'control loss' phenomenon

discussed in the last chapter. Information overloading at the chief executive bottleneck may also lead to gross inefficiency or even collapse of decision-making at this level (Williamson, 1975, p.134).

Secondly, functional executives are liable to have functional rather than profit goals (e.g. sales executives will tend to favour corporate sales rather than return on investment); Chandler observed that a frequent solution to the peak level bottleneck problem was the expansion of strategic decision making capacity by the involvement of functional heads in decision making at this level (Williamson, 1975, p.135). However, given their parochial functional orientation, such involvement is liable to create pressure towards opportunistic pursuit of managerial goals. In such circumstances a managerial utility maximising model (such as that of Williamson, 1964) may be an appropriate description of corporate behaviour (Williamson, 1975, p.150).

Thus, Williamson argues that expansion of the U-form enterprise tends to lead to control loss problems and non-profit maximising behaviour. Simple expansion of existing product lines is sufficient to create these problems eventually, but if growth is by diversification the problems are encountered more rapidly (Williamson, 1971, p.350); each new product requires a minimum package of decision costs and time, and therefore brings with it a quantum step up in information problems.

The typical organisation form solution to these problems is the multidivision corporation (or M-form), of the type illustrated in Fig. 4.2. In this structure, quasi-autonomous operating divisions (organised by product or region) and composed of functional sections, is administered by a general office (assisted by specialist staff for auditing and planning purposes).

As far as the large diversified firm is concerned, the advantages of M-form structure over U-form structure are derived directly from the creation of 'natural decision units'; richly interacting parts are combined and weakly interacting parts are separated (Williamson, 1971, p.356). By joining together at divisional level, strongly inter-related units (whether they have product or regional commonalities) operating decisions can be resolved at divisional level (thus reducing control loss and peak level bottlenecks). General office now has the capacity to specialise in strategic overview and planning of the corporation as a whole, free of distorting functional pressures. (Williamson, 1975, pp.137–8). The staff department provides specialist expertise to general office in the performing of its strategic role.

Therefore, the M-form can help counteract (though not necessarily eliminate) control loss and non-profit objectives of management associated with U-form structure in the large diversified corporation.[8] In those circumstances the M-form provides opportunities for increased internal efficiency, and improved strategic decision making. There is, however, a qualification:

> If the operating divisions are not fully decomposable. . . but experience some modest degree of technical or market interdependency[9] the decoupling. . . cannot be accomplished without cost. Certain of these costs can be attenuated by specification of appropriate inter-divisional rules regarding internal pricing. . . and the like. If these interactions are extensive, however, the information exchange needs of the resulting M-form organisation may be merely different from but not significantly less than its U-form equivalent. Its control-loss experience need not be better and could easily be worse. (Williamson, 1971, pp.357)

Thus, decomposability is an essential prerequisite of the M-form organisation. If we were to consider the three firms in Fig. 3.6 as candidates for divisionalisation, it would seem only Omega would clearly satisfy this precondition. Alpha is highly synergistic with strongly inter-related product-markets, while the links in Beta's case are still substantial. The M-form structure appears to countervene synergy considerations, at least between divisions, by isolating related product markets.

But when, and how, do we determine when an M-form structure is feasible? For example, do we have any means of establishing whether firm Beta can be twisted into a decomposable M-form structure, or whether the attendant control-loss costs across divisions would be too prohibitive? Williamson indicates the pros and cons of U-form and M-form structures in such circumstances, but no systematic basis for relating synergy to internal organisation is provided.

We shall suggest that such a basis can be provided, and in fact is already implicit in Williamson's transaction cost analysis discussed in the previous chapter. In order to develop such a basis we shall first make two simplifying sets of assumptions. *Firstly*, intrafunction links are stronger than interfunction links for a product – e.g. sales managers tend to spend more time talking to each other than to production managers.

This first assumption may seem simple, obvious and innocuous. But it may be extended to imply that if a particular function is fully exploiting all possible synergy links between products, the appropriate intrafunctional links *across* products are strong and inter-functional links *within* products are comparatively weak. The former will require more co-ordination than the latter, e.g. if there was complete or even just high sales synergy, sales executives would spend more time co-ordinating with sales executives in other products, than with other functional executives for the same product.

Secondly, we identify particular transactions costs associated with internal organisation. In the last chapter, the advantages of team organisation versus the market were analysed in terms of reducing the effects of bounded rationality, opportunism and information impactedness. By working shoulder to shoulder, teams could attenuate these costs of arms length market transactions.

However, the U-form and M-form structures are not only hier-achical forms, they are multi-group (or multi-team) forms. Suppose we define each function in the U-form and each division in the M-form as a group; we can now identify three modes of co-ordination; (a) intra-group (b) inter-group (but intra-firm) (c) market.

If intra-group co-ordination is shoulder to shoulder, and market co-ordination is arms length, then inter-group co-ordination approximates to elbow length co-ordination. Group loyalty and inter-group rivalry may encourage opportunism in inter-group co-ordination, though this will not be as severe as in the market place if at least some common corporate interest is recognised and/or head office intervention curbs excessive opportunism (by imposing co-operation or *ex post* sanctions on opportunism). Correspondingly, tendencies towards information impactedness in inter-group co-ordination should not be as great as in market co-ordination, though separation of groups creates inter-group information barriers with a resultant higher level of information impactedness than within groups. Thus, we expect that transaction costs resulting from bounded rationality, opportunism and information impactedness will typically increase as we move from group, to inter-functional or inter-divisional, to market co-ordination.

With the help of these two sets of assumptions, we can now relate synergy maps to internal organisation. It must be emphasised that the following examples are for illustrative purposes only; in practice, detailed analysis of the trade-offs involved in selecting alternative organisation forms would be required. For simplicity we shall assume in each case that the firm requires three functions; sales, manufacturing, R & D. Further, bounded rationality and span of control considerations require that the corporate hierarchy consists of three to four operating groups (i.e. functions and/or divisions) reporting directly to head office (in whose hands is placed the responsibility for strategic decision making). We shall consider five sample firms in turn.

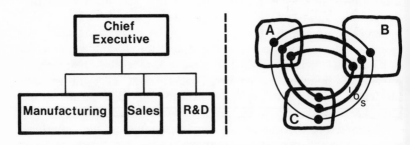

FIGURE 4.3   Internal organisation and synergy map: firm Alpha

We shall begin by suggesting organisation form for firm Alpha, the aluminium sports goods firm discussed in the previous chapter. Synergy links are generally assumed to be complete in Alpha's case, with the exception of weaker sales synergy links between product/market *C* and the rest of the firm. Generally, therefore, strong intra-functional co-ordination is a necessary feature of Alpha's operations. Synergy considerations therefore will tend to dominate relative to the comparatively weaker inter-functional product-market co-ordination problems. Given the need to decompose the firm into three or four groups, transaction costs of bounded rationality, information impactedness and opportunism would be minimised by adopting a U-form structure as in Fig. 4.3. Synergy is exploited at minimal cost by functional executives working shoulder to shoulder, while product-market (inter-functional) co-ordination across groups requires less frequent interaction and incurs some costs of elbow length inter-group transactions. On the other hand, were the firm to be decomposed by activity, the potentially rich synergy transactions would be relatively expensive to conduct. In this case, the U-form structure allows the firm to be decomposed into its natural decision units. However, it should be added that transaction costs considerations alone are not sufficient to determine the choice of organisation form. The superior strategy formulating and internal control properties of the M-form structure add to its advantages compared to the U-form, and must also be taken into account before a choice is made. With this qualification, our analysis may be said to follow in the spirit of Simon (1969); 'hierarchies have the property of near decomposability.[10] Intracomponent linkages are generally stronger than intercomponent linkages' (p.106).[11]

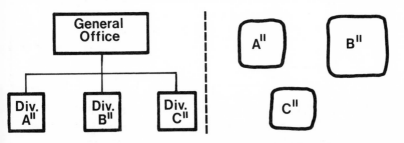

FIGURE 4.4   Internal organisation and synergy map: firm Omega

Firm Omega, the mini-conglomerate, provides a fairly straightforward case. There are no synergy links between activities; however weak inter-functional links still exist for each activity. Co-ordination is therefore best achieved by putting the interacting parts together within a group and organising on an M-form basis as indicated in Fig. 4.4. Further advantages are gained from the strategy formulating and internal control capabilities of the M-form structure.

We shall also consider the third firm (Beta) discussed in Chapter 3, but before doing so, two other distinctive corporate types will be analysed. Firstly, firm Chi is described in Fig. 4.5; Chi is an engineering firm which sells industrial fuel pumps to technologically advanced companies (A'''), agricultural hydraulic pumps to third world countries (B'''), and sewage pumps to public authorities worldwide (C'''). The market and specific design differs significantly in each case; however there is a strong link in each case in terms of the technology of pumping systems.

It could be that manufacturing linkages are strong enough to encourage a fully functional organisational form, but we assume this is not the case in this example. The suggested solution in Fig. 4.5 is a mixed U- and M-form type in so far as R & D exists as a separate function, while A''', B''' and C''' (less R & D in each case) exists as operating divisions. This is an example of Marris' transcendent corporation. Effectively four groups have been created – one with strong internal linkages (R & D) and three with weaker, but

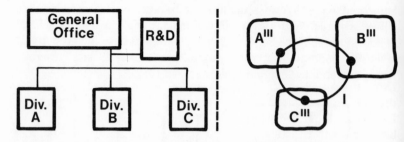

FIGURE 4.5   Internal organisation and synergy map: firm Chi

significant, internal linkages (the activities). Again, natural decision units are created for shoulder-to-shoulder co-ordination.[12]

The organisation structure suggested for firm Chi is a hybrid of U-and M-form structures, with its own peculiar requirements as far as administration and control is concerned. While a transaction cost analysis would seem to suggest the transcendent form as a natural candidate in Chi's case, some reservations may be justified in so far as the different mix of group types (one function, three divisions) may create administrative and control difficulties for the general office.

The fourth firm, firm Pi, is a firm selling lemonade ($\bar{A}$), potato crisps ($\bar{B}$) and chocolate ($\bar{C}$) to children. The market is the same in each case, the technology is assumed to be completely different. The synergy map for Pi, and suggested organisation form, is shown in Fig. 4.6.

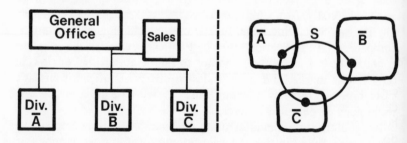

FIGURE 4.6   Internal organisation and synergy map: firm Pi

Pi, as in the other cases discussed above, is separated into natural decision units to minimise the transaction costs of bounded rationality, information impactedness and opportunism. In form, its groups have a construction similar to that of the transcendent corporation

Chi in having one function and three divisions. However, we shall suggest later that there are liable to be different considerations for Chi and Pi relevant to the adoption of the hybrid organisation form in the respective cases.

The final example we shall discuss is that of firm Beta, the third firm introduced in the previous chapter. As made clear in Fig. 4.7 there is no clear cut basis for separating groups in this example. Divisionalisation in Beta's case would sever strong synergy links between the three activities, while functional organisation would only exploit partial synergy links between activities (and would also sacrifice the structure and control benefits of M-form organisation). In contrast to Chi and Pi, there is no strong, consistent synergy link between activities that leads to a specific hybrid form being naturally suggested. In terms of tractability to a suitable organisation form, Beta's strategy presents real problems. The specific form chosen would depend on detailed consideration of costs and benefits of alternative structures.

Organisation Form?

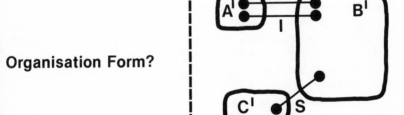

FIGURE 4.7   Internal organisation and synergy map: firm Beta

Thus, the economics of internal organisation and the economics of corporate strategy may be interpreted in the light of a common denominator; transaction costs. The examples above help illustrate how transactional analysis can relate internal organisation to diversification strategies.

However, so far our discussion has been asymmetric; we have considered costs of market transaction systematically, but not costs of organisation. The impression may be taken unjustifiably, that uninhibited expansion of firms is feasible and desirable because of reduction in transaction costs – Williamson, however, redresses the balance for us by identifying three main costs of organisation typically incurred by expansion of the firm. (1975, pp.126–30). Firstly, bounded rationality and finite span of control considerations necessitates additional hierarchical levels if expansion is recurring, leading to associated serial reproduction and control loss problems. Secondly, Williamson argues that increasing size generally leads to a dilution of shareholder power and possibilities for the exercise of managerial discretion, with the resulting inefficiency of organisational slack. Thirdly, impersonality, reduction in intimacy and associated reduction in the relevance of voluntary co-operation, may lead to conflicting or inefficient small group practices as the firm becomes larger and the 'atmosphere' changes.

These organisation costs must be set against costs of using the market in considering the limits to firm size. If the costs of using the market are higher than the costs of internal organisation for all products outwith the boundary of the firm, we would not expect the firm to expand through diversification. If some products or potential products have potential synergy links that could provide a net benefit to the firm, we predict the firm would internalise the product or potential product if effective costs of internal organisation are less than the costs of using the market.[13]

Having explicitly incorporated costs of organisations into our discussion, we can now begin to consider why firms differ in diversification strategy and internal organisation. The central question is the design of the firm in terms of synergy relations, given costs of organisation and markets.

This question can be approached in two stages. Firstly, we would expect the organisation costs of dilution of shareholder power, and change in atmosphere to be a consequence of size *per se*, and independent of the extent to which synergy links exist. Secondly, we would expect the organisation cost of bounded rationality to *decrease* with synergy *ceteris paribus*. This is because the more synergy links that exist, the more familiar will a product be, and the less complex will be the problem facing management (e.g. a diversifying food manufacturer will tend to find it easier to digest a baker than a builder.) However, the more synergy links that exist, so costs of using the market INCREASE *ceteris paribus* (as we argued in the previous chapter). *Given a range of products to choose from then, we would expect the firms combination of activities to exhibit maximum synergy, ceteris paribus.* Synergy is expensive across organisation boundaries, cheap within; as synergy increases, costs of market transaction increase and costs of organisation diminish, *ceteris paribus.*

This is a more complete analysis of the conclusion we reached in the last chapter. We also point out then that firms, in general, *do not* appear to maximise synergy. In the next section we shall discuss why this is the case.

CATASTROPHE AND STRATEGY

Up to this point we have considered the design of corporate strategy solely in terms of synergy benefits. However, this is a purely synchronic approach. We have demonstrated the importance of relations between elements in our static analysis of corporate strategy, but we have argued earlier that synchronic analysis should complement rather than substitute diachronic analysis. Therefore it would appear reasonable, and potentially useful, to consider how we might extend synergy mapping to include diachronic considerations.

We can begin by outlining a tool familiar to managerial economists, the product life cycle. Fig. 4.8 illustrates a typical product life cycle pattern.

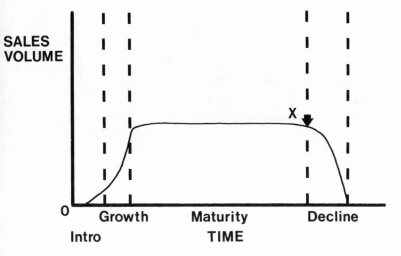

FIGURE 4.8   Product life cycle

In general, a new product will go through a low volume introduction period before entering into the growth period associated with rapid acceleration of sales volume. During the third period, maturity, sales levels stabilise, and finally in the decline phase sales volume diminishes. While length of individual periods, and the shape of the curve, may vary dramatically between products, the general pattern of the product life cycle outlined above tends to be typical. The behaviour of unit profit margins tends to follow a similar cyclical pattern of growth and decline, though casual evidence suggests the peak of this cycle usually occurs during the sales volume growth phase (Clifford, 1976, p.28).

While retaining the concept of life cycle in the analysis below, it is too gross a tool at product level to be applied without modification to the analysis developed here so far. The product life cycle concept is applied to a single product composed of a bundle of characteristics. However individual characteristics may also have their own life cycle implications with relevance to corporate strategy. We can demonstrate this by reference to an example; firm Beta will be used once again for the sake of consistency and simplicity.

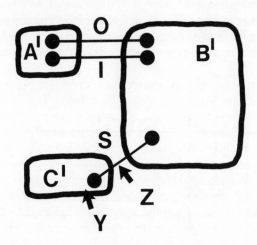

FIGURE 4.9   Firm Beta with environmental threat

Before we consider Fig. 4.9, we shall introduce the concept of a 'catastrophe', which in this context we shall take to mean a phenomenon external to the firm which directly precipitates the decline and obsolescence phase of the product life cycle. In Fig. 4.8 the catastrophe 'X' is represented by a heavy arrow signalling the beginning of decline. We shall consider the general nature of the threat in rather more detail below; for the moment we shall interpret it as providing a *substitute* for the product under attack – for example the aluminium ski was a catastrophe for the wooden ski, while the electronic calculator was a catastrophe for the slide rule.

Our synergy maps outline the synchronic relations at a specific point in time, while the product life cycle concept illustrates dynamic considerations and provides a basis for diachronic analysis, as in the case of the effect of catastrophes on product sales. We can integrate these two aspects in Fig. 4.9; here we assume the synergy map has been constructed at that point in time where a pair of catastrophes, Y and Z, first appear heralding decline in a similar fashion to X in Fig. 4.8. Activity C' in Fig. 4.9 is ski-wear and catastrophe Y may be a new product e.g. ski-wear incorporating a novel, cheap method of insulation. As such it may be expected to have an effect on Beta's ski-wear analogous to the effect of X on product sales in Fig. 4.8.

However, suppose some catastrophic event Z, say, a novel sport, resulted in *ski-ing* declining. What implications would this have for our corporate strategy?

The answer is that it would directly attack the synergy link between B' and C' in Fig. 4.9 since both activities exploit synergy from the ski-ing link on the sales side. In this case B' and C' would decline together.

However, Beta is less vulnerable than Alpha (see Fig. 3.6(a)) to such external assault. Suppose a cheaper and better aluminium alloy was patented and introduced in the sports good arena by a competitor of Alpha. In this case *all* Alpha's activities face the decline phase together since they are linked by the the obsolescing material utilised by Alpha.

It is in this respect that the product life cycle concept operates at too gross a level for the analysis of this chapter. In general we shall assume it is applicable at the level of the *constituent*. In this context constituent is an aspect of activities, examples of which provide sources of synergy when held jointly between activities (see Table 3.1). Thus, distribution channels, inputs and R & D are all examples of constituents. In the examples above, the constituent facing the decline phase is technological in the case of Alpha (aluminium alloy) and sales in the case of Beta (substitute sport). Even in the example of the product life cycle (aluminium skis substituting wooden), the source of catastrophe may be traced down to changes in a specific *constituent* of activity — in this case a material constituent.

Therefore we reinterpret the product life cycle here as the constituent life cycle. Obviously sales volume is no longer a generally applicable measure of intensity of usage of a characteristic; instead the vertical axis in each case will be some appropriate measure of degree of utilisation of the constituent – e.g. volume of inputs, expenditure on advertising, number of machines employed.

By redefining the basic unit of the life cycle concept, we have made this diachronic analysis consistent with the synchronic analysis of synergy maps. As we have defined it, synergy is derivable from *constituents* (see Table 3.1). Transaction costs and costs of organisation are incurred with respect to trading or organising synergy extracted from constituents. Ironically, in extending theory of the firm considerations to the multi-product firm, we have had to develop a more microanalytic approach than is required for the single product firm, and we have done this by establishing the constituent as the basic unit for synchronic and diachronic analysis.

CATASTROPHE AND SYNERGY

So far, synergy has been regarded as an unqualified benefit to the firm. Introducing diachronic analysis changes this interpretation. There are two main costs of synergy when life cycle considerations are introduced, and both are illustrated diagrammatically in Fig. 4.10 for firms operating two activities.

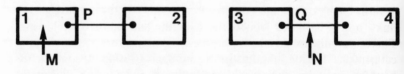

Fig. 4.10(a)   Activity linking   Fig. 4.10(b)   Catastrophe linking

FIGURE 4.10   Catastrophe and synergy

Suppose activity (1) in Fig. 4.10(a) above was faced with a catastrophe M that did not directly affect other activities (a similar example discussed above was catastrophe Y on C' in Fig. 4.9). In such circumstances, activity (1) cannot be considered independently of activity (2) because of the joint effect of shared characteristic P. Consequently divestment of (1) may not be a feasible option for the firm since the viability of (2) may depend on the continued existence and associated synergy benefits of (1). Therefore, the firm's flexibility of response is liable to be severely constrained if there exist synergy elements and joint profitability of activities. This may be a severe problem in risky and uncertain environments where the firm, and its capital become bogged down in highly synergistic but increasingly unprofitable ventures. Synergy therefore trades off against flexibility, as has been emphasised elsewhere by Bradbury *et al* (1973). We describe this as a problem of *activity linking* in Fig. 4.10(a).[14]

Suppose now that two activities face a catastrophe that threatens a shared constituent, as in Fig. 4.10(b) (a similar example above was catastrophe Z on B' and C' in Fig. 4.9). The shared constituent not only provides synergy, it also is now seen to create mutual dependence of the linked activities on the fortunes of that shared constituent. This is described as *catastrophe linking* in Fig. 4.10(b). Catastrophe linking can be a fatal strategy for the firm. For example, Alpha in Fig. 3.6(a) is especially vulnerable to this flaw, particularly in the case of technological constituents. If a major constituent was to face a catastrophe and enter into the decline phase *all* of Alpha's activities would face simultaneous threat, and Alpha's survival would be in severe jeopardy. Firm Beta in Fig. 3.6(b) is also vulnerable to catastrophe linking, but to a lesser extent than Alpha; in this case specific technological catastrophes might jointly affect A' and B', while sales side catastrophes might jointly affect B' and C'. Both the possibility and extent of catastrophe linking is limited to the constituents joined by synergy links in Beta's case.

Firm Omega, the mini-conglomerate in Fig. 3.6(c) has no synergy links, and is insulated from activity linking and catastrophe linking. Therefore vulnerability to both types of linking threat, activity and catastrophe linking, diminishes as number of shared constituents between activities diminishes. Interestingly, introducing diachronic considerations has shown the reverse side of the coin to synchronic analysis; in static analysis of synergy benefits, increasing the number of shared constituents between activities benefited the firm by providing potential synergy gains, while in dynamic analysis increasing the number of shared constituents creates vulnerability to two categories of linking threats, reducing flexibility and creating the possibility of corporate failure through simultaneous decline on a number of fronts.[15] In a synchronic context, Alpha is richer in synergy than Omega; in a diachronic context, Alpha is more vulnerable to linking threat than Omega. The central consideration is that shared constituents is the common denominator for both synchronic and diachronic analysis. The nature of the environment will obviously be crucial in fashioning corporate strategy; a benign, relatively static type environment should encourage Alpha type firms, while a turbulent, catastrophe laden type environment should encourage Omega type firms.

We now are in a position to present casual explanations as to why Alpha, Beta, and Omega adopt their respective strategies. Synergy is not a free good, and its price increases with the frequency and importance of catastrophe. The different strategies of Alpha, Beta and Omega are *environmentally* determined since we assume the natural inclination of firms is to maximise synergy in the expected absence of catastrophe. This obviously highlights the nature of catastrophic events as a major problem in analysis of corporate strategy. We reserve fuller discussion of this to the next chapter.

THE SYNERGY BOND

We conclude this chapter with a reconsideration of the role of the theory of the firm, and the relevance of the concepts of synergy and catastrophe. P.W.S. Andrews (1964) states the problem clearly:

> An analysis of the orthodox kind, that proceeds from analyses in terms of single products to conclusion which invite or thrust upon us applications to 'firms' as we know them, should surely have considered how the combination of products might affect the relative position of businesses. (pp.87-8)

It should, but it has not. It has been suggested here that delving down to the level of the transaction facilitates analysis of the multiproduct firm. However, in doing so, a picture of the firm radically different from that of neoclassical theory has been developed. In Chapter 2 a comparison was drawn between thermodynamic models and neoclassical theory; it was suggested that what the theory of the firm lacked was analysis of synchronic relations as in the science of chemistry. In fact the construction of synergy maps has resulted in models of the corporation bearing a resemblance to description of chemical compounds; instead of atoms joined by chemical bonds, synergy maps describe activities joined by synergy links. Can we interpret these synergy links as bonds in an analogous sense to chemical bonds?

We can do so, but the strength of the bond should not be measured directly in terms of synergy benefits. As has been argued earlier, the firm and the market place are alternative modes of co-ordinating synergy; if the market costs are high in terms of exploiting synergy, we would expect a correspondingly strong 'bond' between the respective activities within the firm. On the other hand, if market costs of organising synergy benefits were lower than organisation costs, these would be a negative 'bond' between activities within the firm. In short, the strength of the bond between activities within the firm may be measured as the *opportunity cost* for respective activities if they were to be co-ordinated by the market place rather than the firm; the opportunity cost would be measured in synergy sacrificed and extra cost in extracting synergy by the market.

Therefore, with some justification, it may be said that the approach developed here is as distinctive from neoclassical theory as is chemistry from thermodynamics – and for similar reasons. However, in emphasising the importance of the synchronic relations here, it must also be borne in mind that diachronic factors are an essential part of this analysis. We shall integrate both features in the next chapter.

CONCLUSION

This chapter has consolidated the theoretical development of the last chapter. Previous work of Kay (1979) was briefly considered using Piaget's structuralist categories and compared with the present analysis. There were two strong parallels with the present analysis; firstly it was strongly argued in the previous work that diachronic and synchronic analysis was complementary, that is dynamic adjustment processes as in behavioural theory could lead to a hierarchical system of resource preferences through a process of learning; secondly the structuralist perspective of both this and the previous work directly contradicted the aggregative approach of neoclassical theory.

It was suggested that both approaches could be integrated within one framework, after which possible relationships between synergy maps and internal organisation were examined. Previous studies have argued that strategy determines structure, and synergy maps permit systematic analysis of these relationships. A second main theoretical development of this chapter was the integration of synchronic and diachronic analysis in the present work. Diachronic analysis was embodied in the adjustment processes and causal relations of the product life cycle, while synchronic relations were represented by static synergy links. Past studies have to concern themselves with one or other of these concepts considered in isolation; product life cycle implications have been usually analysed without reference to synergy considerations, and vice versa. A contribution here is to suggest how both concepts may be regarded as respective sides of a coin called corporate strategy.

5 Choice of Strategy

We have arrived at the stage where we can begin to tie threads together to build models of corporate behaviour based on the structuralist theory developed in the earlier chapters. Here we shall construct a simple model of firm decision-making which we shall apply in the chapters following in an examination of some problems in industrial organisation. It should be borne in mind throughout that we are looking from the point of view of decision-makers (managerial) rather than owners (shareholders).

Our analysis suggests synergy and environmental change as important determinants of diversification strategy. Theories already exist identifying both factors as being of relevance to diversification. In terms of environmental effects, portfolio theory is the standard approach to diversification problems, and has been cited as an alternative to synergy based approaches (e.g. Weston, 1970). The first section of this chapter argues that portfolio theory should be discounted as an explanation of firm strategy. The remainder of the chapter is concerned with the development of a structuralist theory of the firm.

We introduce portfolio theory at this stage of the analysis for a very sound reason. In the previous chapter we introduced the concept of environmental variability determining corporate strategy; portfolio theory is an existing theory which already performs this function. Consequently, before we develop our framework further,it is important to consider the possible relevance of this approach; there is little point in rediscovering the effect of environmental variability on strategy if portfolio theory already has the answers, as some analysts of corporate diversification do indeed believe.

In fact it will be argued that portfolio theory is not a particularly useful approach in analysing corporate strategy and that the effect of environmental variation has to be considered in the context of product life cycles rather than an inappropriate theory rooted in financial analysis.

ENVIRONMENT AND STRATEGY

Portfolio theory analyses the financial effects of diversifying investments. Profitability and risk are the two main concerns of this
approach, with profit providing a source of utility to the investor and
risk providing a source of disutility. Although the approach was
originally developed for application to the holding of financial assets,[1]
it has been extended to business strategy (e.g. see Weston, 1970).
Recently portfolio theory has been modified to recognise the
possibility of debtor default, or bankruptcy. We shall discuss these
developments in the next chapter, but first we shall consider the
relevance of standard portfolio theory to corporate diversification.

According to standard portfolio theory as developed by Markowitz
(1952, 1959), we can interpret investment as relating to financial assets
or to actual activities. Using this approach we can investigate the
implications of a diversified portfolio of financial assets, or effects of
corporate diversification. In both cases, if two investments are held by
the individual or institution then,

$$E(\pi_{st}) = E(\pi_{1t}) + E(\pi_{2t}) \tag{1}$$

where $E(\pi_{1t})$, $E(\pi_{2t})$ is the expected profit in time t for investment 1,
investment 2 respectively, $E(\pi_{st})$ is total expected profit in time t.

This assumes there is no interaction between investments; obviously
if synergy benefits were extracted, total expected profit would be
greater than the simple sum of investments considered separately. It is
this effect on expected profit that leads to the colloquial interpretation
of synergy as the '2 + 2 = 5 effect' (Ansoff, 1965, pp. 72–5).

In those circumstances, the standard deviation for the financial
combination is

$$\sigma_{st} = \sqrt{(\sigma_{1t}^2 + 2r_t\sigma_{1t}\delta_{2t} + \sigma_{2t}^2)} \tag{2}$$

where σ_{1t}, σ_{2t} is the standard deviation in profit in time t for
investment 1 and investment 2 respectively. r_t is the correlation
coefficient between expected profit levels of investment 1 and
investment 2.[2] The standard deviation for the combination is *not* the
sum of individual standard deviations, but is instead a function of
individual standard deviations and the correlation between expected
profit levels. We can illustrate the implications of portfolio
diversification by reference to a simple example.[3] Assume first of all

that we are operating two independent firms, with $E(\pi_{1t}) = E(\pi_{2t}) =$ \$1 million, and $\sigma_{1t} = \sigma_{2t} =$ \$400,000. If we now merge the two firms into one corporation, we can take the coefficient of variation – this is $\sigma_{st}/E(\pi_{st})$ for the combination – as a measure of *risk*. This measure shows the importance of profit variability relative to the expected level of profits. If the plants are operating separately, the coefficient of variation is 40 per cent in each case.

The level of risk for the combination depends crucially on the correlation between profit levels. If correlation is perfectly negative ($r_t = -1.0$), then the coefficient of variation is zero. Deviations in profitability in one plant are exactly offset by compensating deviations in the other. If, on the other hand, profit variability in plant 1 is completely unrelated to profit variability in plant 2 (i.e. $r_t = 0$), the coefficient of variation is only 28 per cent, compared to the 40 per cent for separately operated plants.[4] A third extreme case obtains if there is perfect correlation between profits ($r_t = 1.0$). In this case the coefficient of variation for the combination is 40 per cent, the same as for the case of separate plants.

As long as there is not perfect positive correlation in profits between the two plants, the coefficient of variation will be less for the combination than for the plants if operated independently. Thus diversification reduces risk as long as $r_t \neq 0$.

Since coefficient of variation, the measure of risk, tends to decline as r_t declines, we might expect to find risk averters diversifying into unrelated markets to smooth variations in earnings. In this connection, we would expect to find a direct relation between r_t and the extent of synergy links; the more common links in the form of shared constituents, the higher r_t, *ceteris paribus*. For example if the shared constituent is technological (say, aluminium alloy) variations in its cost should have proportional effects on the operating costs of the respective plants, while if the shared constituent is on the sales side (say, both plants supply the ski market), then revenue conditions of the respective plants should vary together to some extent. In the case of complete or perfect links between constituents we would expect $r_t = 1$.[5]

This appears to suggest portfolio theory as the natural complement to synergy since increasing the level of shared constituents has two effects, *ceteris paribus*; firstly it increases the joint expected profitability of combination, secondly it increases the associated level of risk of combination. The first is a source of utility to owners of the firm, the second is a source of disutility. Since both are directly related to the degree of relatedness between constituents (measured in terms of number of shared constituents), diversification strategy for corporate management would seem to be a problem of balancing the synergy benefits of increasing level of activity relatedness against the costs of increased risk. The respective approaches can be interpreted at the level of the constituent.

However, the view if taken here that portfolio theory in this form has little, if any, relevance to problems of corporate diversification. We shall argue this by introducing a simple multiperiod period problem for an activity (say, plant 1 above) such that

$$E(\pi_t) = \phi \tag{3}$$
$$\sigma(\pi_t) = \delta \tag{4}$$
$$L_t = \pi_t - E(\pi_t) \tag{5}$$
$$\therefore E(L_t) = 0 \text{ (from (3) and (5))}.$$

(*Note* $t = 1 \ldots N$
ϕ = constant
δ = constant)

In our example we assume that π_t varies as in the diagram below; expected profit level and profit variance are both constant for all time periods, and so therefore is the coefficient of variation, or level of risk. There is no correlation between expected profit levels of any time periods. We ignore the trend line π_t for the moment.

In Fig. 5.1 actual profit varies around the expected level of profit from time period to time period. Now, once multiperiod considerations are introduced for plant 1, a range of potential actions may be

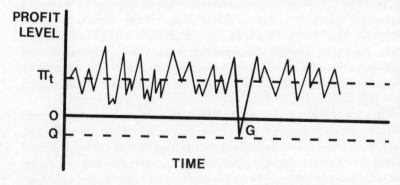

FIGURE 5.1　Multi-period risk

open to the firm with respect to risk reduction. Forward contracts may be agreed with buyers and/or suppliers,[6] stockholding may reduce variability of prices of inputs,[7] and vertical integration may reduce vulnerability to short term fluctuations in market conditions.[8] Each of these solutions may reduce profit variability by reducing variability of supply, output and/or prices.[9] These are possibilities which are not generally recognised in portfolio theory, essentially because it is a single period financial theory and not a multiperiod theory of the firm.

However, there is a further criticism of the application of portfolio theory to corporate diversification strategy in so far as once multiperiod considerations are recognised, the firm may be regarded as diversifying risk over time. For N time periods, the coefficient of variation of total profit over that period is $\delta/\sqrt{N}$. As N increases, the coefficient of variation tends to zero.[10] For large N, risk effectively disappears. It still exists for individual time periods, but the firm could subsidise short term shortfalls (negative L_t in equation (5) above) by going to the capital market and using its effectively risk free long term prospects as security to support losses (e.g. G in Fig. 5.1).

A problem here is transaction costs. In particular, an information impactedness condition might exist in favour of the firm and against the capital market in terms of the firms true prospects (e.g. see Williamson, 1975, pp.155–75). In such circumstances the market may be reluctant to support the firm without extracting expensive premiums, if at all. However if the multiperiod conditions above do hold, the firm has everything to gain by making information freely available to a reputable source of finance. In this case openness and not opportunism best serves the firm, and it should endeavour to break down the information barrier between it and the potential source of short term funds.[11] This should have a corresponding beneficial effect on transaction costs of short term funding. Therefore, extending the simple problem above to a multiperiod one indicates other opportunities for dealing with risk other than diversification. These techniques may have associated costs in each case; how may they compare with diversification in this respect?

The view is taken here that corporate diversification to reduce risk will be generally prohibitively expensive compared to other alternatives. This is because corporate diversification to reduce risk involves a cost not incurred in financial portfolio diversification – loss of potential synergy benefits. Suppose the firm faces a range of activities it can incorporate within its walls, each with the same expected level of profit and required capital investment when considered independently; in those circumstances diversifying to spread risk will generally be effective to the extent that activity relatedness is avoided and synergy sacrificed. Risk reduction is achieved but its price is synergy, a potentially extremely expensive trade. On the other hand, if the firm was to diversify into synergy rich areas, the only capital market cost incurred would be in terms of the transaction costs of obtaining capital market support in lean times.[12]

Multiperiod solutions are generally not thought of as being very interesting in portfolio theory; as Champernowne (1969) points out:

> there is no very great gain to be made from a multiperiod analysis of portfolio decisions, since it is possible at the next annual review to start all over again, and after all switches are not prohibitively expensive. (p.27–8)

This is the case in financial diversification; it is not liable to be the case in corporate diversification where the partial bonding together of activities resulting from the pursuit of synergy creates inter-relationships and entanglements at operating level, with associated inflexibility of resources. Corporations cannot change direction as easily as portfolios. Synergy meshes activities, and a multiperiod horizon is necessary to cope with this problem.

However we have previously suggested that variability due to changes in the environment must be taken into account. Here we have argued that corporate diversification is generally an expensive method of dealing with risk caused by environmental variation, and suggested other methods may be preferable in most circumstances. In the next section we shall suggest how environmental change may encourage diversification.

LIFE CYCLE AND CATASTROPHE

It is suggested in this section that, as far as corporate diversification is concerned, the important consideration is not risk but instead the possibility of a decline in the level of expected profit of corporate activities. Fig. 5.2 illustrates this argument. *OABC* is a constituent life cycle facing catastrophe at point *B*. The catastrophe is in fact a constituent innovation, part of whose life cycle is illustrated (*DEF*). Fig. 5.1 is represented as the maturity stage of the constituent life cycle

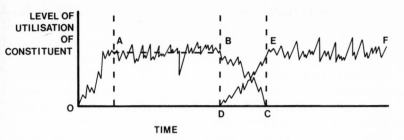

FIGURE 5.2   Creative destruction in constituent life cycles

(*AB*). The maturity phase is more likely to approximate to the stable $E(\pi_{1t})$ assumption of the multiperiod risk example discussed in the previous section.

Suppose all activities of the firm employ this constituent. How might we expect corporate techniques to deal with environmental variability to change in the course of the life cycle?

If we take the maturity phase first, environmental variation in this case is entirely of the risk type discussed in the previous section. We would expect stockholding, forward contracts, vertical integration and/or capital market support to be adequate solutions. As far as the introduction and growth phases are concerned (*OA*) the upward trend in the cycle should make it easier for the firm to bear or mitigate risk; for example the growth trend should encourage the capital market to fund short term shortfalls.[13] We could go even further and suggest that if these methods are not used it may simply reflect low disutility of risk in multiperiod analysis.

However in the decline phase, the relevance of these techniques diminishes. Forward contracts and stockholding are based on *existing* technology and markets. The firm would not wish to hold stocks or agree future prices of an obsolescing input nor would it be likely to find suitable buyers willing to guarantee future prices of an obsolescing output. Vertical integration constitutes an extension of existing technology and therefore merely extends the range of the activity trend into a declining constituent, while capital market support will typically be difficult to obtain for existing activities if major constituents are obsolescing.

Depending on circumstances, each of these solutions could still contribute towards the reduction or elimination of risk in the decline phase. However the important feature of the decline phase is not risk but catastrophe. None of these solutions can inhibit decline since they retain the obsolescing constituent. It is in this context that diversification becomes a relevant consideration.

In contrast to the other solutions, diversification provides real benefits in the face of catastrophe. It was argued in the last chapter that activity linking and catastrophe linking were costs of synergy if the environment produces threats to constituent survival; the corollary here is that the costs of diversification (sacrifice of potential synergy) decrease as threat of catastrophe increases.

The reasons for this is that diversification reduces dependence on the fortunes of individual constituents. If, as we have assumed, all activities share the constituent now facing decline, then all the activities of the firm will be adversely affected, and individual activities will each enter into the decline phase.[14] Catastrophe linking threatens the viability of the whole firm, not just individual activities. On the other hand diversification into loosely related or unrelated areas dilutes the effects of catastrophe by its creation of variety and differentiation in the constituents of activites. This, then, is the real opportunity afforded by corporate diversification in that it may reduce the possibility of simultaneous obsolescence of the firm's activities on all fronts at once. If the firm was faced with all, or even most, of its activities failing at the same time, bankruptcy is a likely outcome. Thus, diversification into differentiated activities offers opportunities for coping with potential catastrophe by reducing or eliminating activity and catastrophe linking.

In case this section appears to be labouring points that are obvious from preceding discussion, it should be emphasised that we have arrived at a major and radical conclusion. Potential variability due to risk has no effect on corporate diversification; potential variability due to catastrophe stimulates corporate diversification. These are held as hypotheses and are at variance with conventional portfolio theory as to the objectives of corporate diversification.[15]

As far as specifying the nature of catastrophe further, Fig. 5.2 does this diagrammatically. Catastrophe is taken to be the appearance of novel substitutes for existing constituents. Technological change is the source of catastrophe. Thus, in Fig. 5.2, the introduction of the constituent innovation (point *D*) is the catastrophe for the existing innovation. The constituent innovation in this example eventually replaces the original constituent entirely (point *E*). This process can be regarded as a type of creative destruction similar to that described by Schumpeter (1942, pp.81–6). As in Schumpeter's argument, the innovation displaces the existing phenomenon, the 'creative' aspect being the innovation development over *DE* and the 'destruction' being decline of existing constituent over *BC*. The difference is that Schumpeter's argument relates to the growth and decay of product-markets rather than constituents.[16]

However we face a further problem at this point. As long as we are dealing with problems of static technology in a stochastic environment then portfolio risk theories based on 'measurable uncertainty' (Knight, 1921) may be invoked to explain risky decision-making. However, we have argued that diversification into poorly related areas is not undertaken to reduce risks in conditions of static technology. Instead, the relevant concern relates to decline in profitability in individual product lines at some indeterminate point in the future; the firm will be 'mugged' by exogenous technological change leading to the decline phase of the constituent life cycle. However, by virtue of its very definition, innovation is a unique event and therefore the incidence, effect and extent of exogenous technological change will be characterised by 'unmeasurable uncertainty' (Knight, 1921). How do we cope with this aspect of life cycle management?

Since innovation is a unique event, we do not suggest how the management of the firm might make probability estimates of individual environmental technological changes that might affect the viability of specific activities. Rather, all we expect of the firm's management is that it recognises that certain activities operate in environments with a higher level of technological change compared to other activities (e.g. electronics compared to textiles). Given the number of shared constituents, a higher incidence of environmental threats will increase the global level of threat to corporate survival due to potential levels of technological change, potential catastrophe and threat to corporate survival will all be assumed measurable in ordinal terms.

Therefore, to summarise, technological change represents a threat to the viability of corporate activities. It is unexpected in terms of when, and in what form, it will occur. However, activities can be identified as belonging to environments that may be ordered in terms of level of technological change and vulnerability to catastrophe.

We hypothesise that firms will attempt to deal with the problem of environmental technological change by *hedging*. We define hedging here as precisely the negation of synergy – it is achieved by reducing the number of shared constituents between corporate activities, and so reducing the extend of activity linking and catastrophe linking.

In the next section we shall develop a simple model built around the synergy and hedging aspects of corporate strategy

CORPORATE STRATEGY

We shall introduce two variables to deal with the characteristics of corporate strategy. Firstly, we shall define a measure of the degree of activity relatedness indicating the extent to which activities share constituents. It is simple to give casual examples of high and low activity relatedness; a conglomerate obviously has a low degree of activity relatedness, while a specialised food company operates with a high degree of activity relatedness. Further, when we look at empirical studies in the later chapters, classification of diversified firms along a broad spectrum of activity relatedness is generally quite possible, for example, a number of studies we shall look at classify firms by unrelated/related/dominated and single product strategies, and it is generally reasonable to assume that this ordering of strategies is in the direction of increasing activity relatedness. Other studies will be looked at which measure diversification in a number of ways, such as simple industry count of industries in which the firm is involved, or level of employment devoted to other than the firms primary industry. Both these measures may be taken as indicators of the extent to which activities are unrelated. The classification systems in each case provide crude measures of activity relatedness.

In some respects this is quite adequate. In our analysis here, we will be concerned with the problem of whether or not we can identify broad patterns of resource allocation, at the level of the economy. Precise measure of activity relatedness represents a luxury as far as our purposes are concerned, since obtaining unambiguous and operational measures of activity relatedness or diversification is a problem that has traditionally bedevilled analysts in this area. For example, if two firms have different mixes of shared constituents, how do we rate or rank activity relatedness? There is a genuine problem of measurement and comparability in this area.

On the other hand it is desirable that some degree of rigour be imposed on our interpretation of activity relatedness, both to guard against possible ambiguity in our analysis, and as a guide to future formal model-building. Consequently we will assume that there is a consistent order in which links between constituents are established; that is, if a constituent is shared for X per cent of the firm's output in a certain strategy, strategies involving equal of higher levels of activity relatedness also have this shared constituent for X per cent of the firm's output. This gives us an unambiguous basis for comparing degree of activity relatedness associated with different strategies; we define activity relatedness as r, an ordinal measure ranging from 0 (no shared constituents between activities) to 1 (perfect or complete sharing of constituents between activities). We can assume that the firm is large enough such that no activity contributes a significant proportion of the firm's business. However this does not preclude the single product firm ($r = 1$) which is the case of perfect or complete sharing of constituents between all activities.[17]

Fig. 5.3 illustrates strategies of varying degrees of activity relatedness using categories of constituents from Table 3.1 and Fig. 3.5(a). For simplicity we shall use alternative strategies open to a small three-activity firm; we break our stricture on activities not representing a significant proportion of firm's business for illustrative purposes.

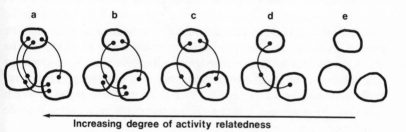

Increasing degree of activity relatedness

FIGURE 5.3 Strategies with varying degrees of activity relatedness

Activity relatedness increases from right to left in Fig. 5.3. Two points merit emphasis and clarification. Firstly, although we specify strategies involving equal levels of activity relatedness share the same constituent for X per cent of their business, the *form* the constituent takes may differ between the two cases. For example, the shared constituent may be R & D in both strategies; but the R & D may be, say, chemical R & D in one case, and mechanical R & D in the other. Secondly, we have expressed activity relatedness in terms of proportionality; the size of the firm is not a relevant consideration here, instead it depends on the proportion of the shared constituents between alternative strategies. We shall return to the question of size of firm later in the chapter.

The second variable we shall introduce here, p, is a measure of the expected degree of environmental technological change. In this formulation, we assume that the firm chooses activities that have the same associated catastrophe potential, and that the consequent p factor characterises the whole strategy. Again p is measured in ordinal terms; if $p = 0$ this is the case where environmental technological change is not expected at all, while if $p = 1$ the imminent obsolence of all constituents is continually anticipated.

Our firm adopts a strategy *Srp*, where the subscripts denote the appropriate degrees of activity relatedness and environmental technological change associated with the activities.

We now define a utility function for management:

U = utility derivable from *Srp* in period j ($j = 1 \ldots m$)

π^* = a variable representing level of return on capital employed in period j

C = a variable representing the perceived level of environmental threat to corporate survival in period j.

The reason that the profitability measure is asterisked is to indicate that it is measured in *ordinal* terms and not cardinally. The management can compare strategies ordinally in terms of expected profitability, but does not estimate precise percentage return on investment figures.

We shall express our utility function as follows:

$$\max U = (\pi^*)$$
$$\text{subject to } C \leq \phi$$
$$\text{where } \phi \text{ is a constant and } (\delta U / \delta \pi^*) > 0.$$

We assume that the firm maximises profitability subject to a survival constraint. A tolerable level of survival potential is the prime objective of the firm, and once satisfied, profitability is pursued. This is a management utility function, and we leave open the question of the uses to which profitability is put; it may be used to pay dividends, pursue growth or other managerial motives.

However we can also express profitability and catastrophe potential as functions of r and p. Firstly profitability:

$$\pi^* = g\,(r,\ p)$$
$$\text{where } (\delta \pi^* / \delta r) > 0,\ (\delta \pi^* / \delta p) > 0.$$

From our previous argument we expect that the synergy benefits of increasing activity relatedness would increase the level of expected profitability, *ceteris paribus*. However we also assume that if the firm is willing to move into a more hostile environment in terms of increased propensity to generate catastrophes, this has a positive effect on the level of anticipated profitability. This may be regarded as a premium for catastrophe potential analogous to a premium for risk taking. We interpret π^* as an ordinal measure simply because all we require of management is that they can distinguish environments in terms of catastrophe potential, and that they associate higher levels of profitability with more hostile environments. Requiring cardinal estimation of profitability is a stronger and unnecessary condition.

As far as the relation between catastrophe potential and r, p is concerned we assume:

$$C = h\,(r,\,p)$$
$$\text{where } (\delta C/\delta r) > 0,\ (\delta C/\delta p) > 0.$$

As we would expect from our previous analysis, increasing r increases vulnerability to activity and catastrophe linking problems, *ceteris paribus*, while increasing p also increases the perceived level of environmental threat, *ceteris paribus*.

However there is one possibility we have ignored so far, and that relates to the implications of interdependence between π^* and C. We assume here that π^* and C can be regarded as independent components of the utility function. In reality, increases in π^* may be expected to be reflected in reduced C due to the expected buffer of slack resources, while increased C is liable to reduce π^* to the extent there is increased frequency of declining activities.

We shall assume these effects may be ignored for present purposes. This may be seen to be more reasonable if we compare the effects of technological change to the emergency stop of a driving test. Just as the emergency stop may not greatly affect driving speed over the course of the test, so we assume that π^* in multiperiod analysis will not be greatly affected by the switch of corporate resources necessitated by the effects of technological change. As with emergency stops, the firm cannot anticipate when they will occur, only that some environments will tend to be associated with stronger and/or more frequent effects of the activity linking and catastrophe linking type. We can illustrate this by reference to Fig. 5.2. The 'emergency stop' phase corresponds to the interval over DC in this case. We presume that this phase is short enough for its effects on profitability to be ignored. The important consideration for the firm is whether a sufficiently high proportion of its activities are forcing 'emergency stop' for its survival to be threatened, and this is where synergy and catastrophe potential is important.

As far as effects in the other direction, from π^* to C, are concerned we shall assume that the firm plans on retention of a fixed amount as liquid reserves (including current earnings) in each time period.[18] Thus, over m time periods of a multiperiod analysis, in any period the firm will have a fixed capability as far as the drain on liquid reserves caused by the (relatively) short, sharp, switching effects of technological change is concerned.

Therefore we may confirm the utility function as:[19]

$$\max U = g\,(r,\,p)$$
$$\text{subject to } h\,(r,\,p) \leq \phi$$

Both profitability and catastrophe are functions of activity relatedness and environmental technological change. We can examine the behaviour implied by the above utility function by constructing Fig. 5.4. Fig. 5.4 illustrates the range of strategies open to a firm with p varying along the vertical axis from a completely static environment to a state of continual change, and r varying from completely unrelated to perfectly related activities along the horizontal axis.

We can consider corporate behaviour by considering the survival and profitability motives in turn. Firstly we can examine the characteristics of the survival constraint; since we have assumed $(\delta C/\delta r) > 0$ and $(\delta C/\delta p) > 0$ we can vary corporate strategy to maintain a binding constraint by trading off p for r, or vice versa, such that $C = \phi$. For example, if $C = \phi$, and we wish to increase r, we may assume that in general there exists some reduced value of p which will maintain $C = \phi$. Therefore there is a negative slope to the survival constraint (ZZ') in Fig. 5.5 caused by this r/p trade-off.

If we construct indifference curves for the contribution alternative strategies make to profitability, a similar negative slope is obtained for indifference curves. Since $(\delta\pi^*/\delta r) > 0$ and $(\delta\pi^*/\delta p) > 0$, the same level of utility and expected profitability can be maintained by trading off catastrophe premium for synergy; that is reducing p and simultaneously increasing r, or vice versa. Thus, our indifference curves have a negative slope, though they are not necessarily convex, for example XX' and YY' in Fig. 5.4. Utility and expected profitability increases as we attain higher indifference curves moving from the bottom left hand corner in Fig. 5.4 where activity relatedness are both zero; for example, utility increases along the line *VW*.

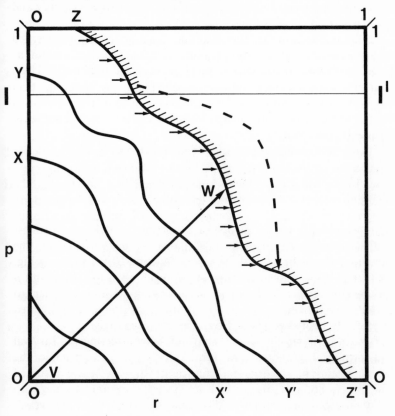

FIGURE 5.4 Corporate behaviour

As far as the problem of where the firm will operate on *ZZ'* is concerned, we can deal with this by explicitly introducing competition into our analysis and assuming that firms have the same utility function, that is they maximise profits subject to a shared valuation of threat to corporate survival, ϕ. In such circumstances we predict that differences in π^* along *ZZ'* will attract entrants to the high profit *Srp* and encourage exit from the low profit *Srp*. As long as there is a finite set of activities associated with each *Srp*, the process of entry and exit should erode differences in profitability until they are equalised along *ZZ'*.

This is a rather strong assumption which we would expect would be modified in later analysis by bringing in the possibility of barriers to entry. In particular, in the next chapter we shall be concerned with industry level analysis at 2-digit level in the US, and we would expect the knowledge barrier across industry boundaries to permit differences in profitability along the survival constraint. If it is reasonable to assume that all activities in certain industry have a constant level of p associated with them, then the firm will be able to vary r much more easily than it will p.[20] Thus, shifts in strategy will typically tend to be in the direction indicated in Fig. 5.4 by the horizontal arrows,[21] with horizontal bands such as II′ representing broadly defined industries.

There is a question that has only been touched on briefly so far, and that is the problem of firm size. The view is taken here that as long as the firm is large enough for individual activities not to dominate decision making (i.e. tactics and strategy can be carried out at separate levels without tactics directly impinging on the 'sphere of operation' of strategy) then *size of firm is unimportant*.

The reasons for this can be illustrated by taking as example, a firm already discussed (say, firm Beta). Suppose Beta faced a competitor Beta-Two in each of its three markets, that is identical in all respects except one. Beta-Two is 4 times bigger in each of its product markets (see Fig. 5.5). In this case, expected profitability of Beta-Two would be greater than Beta (measured in terms of level of expected profitability relative to capital employed),[22] while the severity of impact of specific catastrophes (say $\bar{C}$) would be the same *in relative terms* for Beta-Two as for Beta. The overall vulnerability of Beta-Two to environmental threat is the same as Beta.

What is important as far as relative profitability and vulnerability to catastrophe is concerned is the *pattern* of links, not size of corporation. This assertion may seen difficult to accept as first, but it follows naturally from the analysis developed here. After a point, size confers no survival benefits, a diversified 'little 'un' will be a safer bet than a specialised 'big 'un' in the same industry. Synergy does not provide a buffer against environmental threat since profits are not kept in liquid form due to potential take-over threat. Therefore we would expect both Beta *and* Beta-Two to be knocking against the same survival constraint at the same point. Beta-Two may obtain higher levels of synergy (in the form of economies of scale for identical activities here) but the environmental threat is the same in both cases. There is no internal contradiction in our model in permitting different firms to co-exist in the same market with different levels of

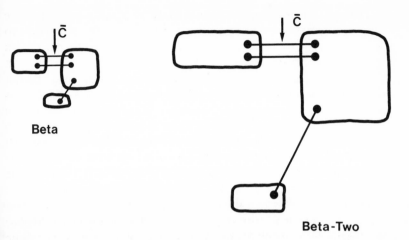

Beta

Beta-Two

FIGURE 5.5   Beta and Beta-Two

profitability since ours is a managerial utility function; e.g. the higher profitability of Beta-Two may be absorbed as slack rather than used to exploit a competitive advantage over Beta.

CONCLUSION

This chapter has developed what may be the simplest possible formal model based on the theoretical argument of the previous two chapters. Its purpose is to show that the approach developed here is amenable to such treatment; the model chosen should not be regarded as the last word, but only one chosen from many possibilities. At this point in our work we could have decided to pursue a case level approach based on synergy maps, or moved in the direction of more abstract theorising for the purpose of analysing resource allocation questions. The first alternative is an interesting one for future analysis, but we have chosen to pursue the latter course in the remainder of this work. For the purposes of developing the theoretical base of the previous two chapters, our primary objective in this chapter was to show that formal development is feasible in the first instance; we obviously hope to demonstrate in the remaining chapters that it is also useful, but for the moment our concern is with exploring methods by which formal technique and analytical tools can be fashioned. We leave open the possibility that retooling may be required, and indeed we would be surprised if further modification turned out to be unnecessary.

6 Diversification Strategy

This chapter will base its examination of aspects of the diversification problem on existing analyses. We shall start by using data from a number of existing studies in looking at patterns of diversification in relation to technological change. Then we shall look briefly at the extent of R & D diversification in different US industries. The next section is concerned with relations between industrial inventive activity and diversification, and the third section is concerned with examination of the portfolio risk theory of diversification; in both cases puzzles thrown up by empirical studies are discussed in the light of the approach developed earlier.

Therefore, the chapter falls naturally into three sections, though of unequal length and importance. One difficulty is differences in interpretation of the concept of diversification; some studies favour industry count or industry specialisation measures, while others favour analysis of the form of diversification in terms of the exten to which links between activities are identifiable. The obvious preference in this analysis is for the latter interpretation, though we hope to demonstrate the generality of our framework by usefully re-examining studies based on the former interpretation.

To start with, we look at patterns of diversification in the context of synergy opportunities and threat of catastrophe

PATTERNS OF DIVERSIFICATION

In looking at the determinants of diversification strategy below, a set of related studies will be particularly useful. In the early 1970s the Harvard Business School sponsored a co-ordinated research programme in which a number of researchers investigated corporate strategy and structure in different countries for their respective doctoral dissertations. The results have been published in Rumelt (1974), Channon (1973) and Dyas and Thanheiser (1976). Rumelt's thesis provides the most useful format for our purposes, and so we shall begin by looking at this investigation of the strategy and structure of US industry.

Using a sample of 246 firms randomly drawn from the Fortune 500, Rumelt conducted tests on the sample for the years 1949, 1959, and 1969. Each firm was assessed in terms of the strategy it followed in particular year, as estimated by Rumelt. In assessing strategy, three measures were used by Rumelt:[1] (a) specialisation ratio (S.R.), defined as the proportion of the firm's revenues attributable to its largest specific product-market; (b) related ratio (R.R.), defined as the proportion of the firm's revenues attributable to the largest group of businesses that were related to each other. Each member of the group needed to be related to only one other business in the group (*linked* relatedness), though there could be a specific skill or strength common to all businesses in this group (*constrained* relatedness);[2] (c) vertical ratio (V.R.) defined as the proportion of a firm's revenues attributable to all the stages of a vertically integrated sequence of operation. In particular, Rumelt distinguished between dominant businesses that were vertically integrated and those that were not. However, the determinants of vertical integration are not necessarily the same as diversification (as our earlier analysis suggests). Accordingly, no distinction is made here between completely homogenous activities (single product-market), and vertically integrated activity having a homogenous final output. Consequently, we combine the two categories in our analysis.

Rumelt distinguished five major categories of corporate strategy by product-market; single, dominant, related-constrained, related-linked and unrelated. Single business firms had specialisation ratios of .95 or greater. Dominant firms had specialisation ratios of between .7 and .95. Related firms all had specialisation ratios of less than .7 but related ratios of greater than .7. Unrelated firms had related ratios of less than .7.

In the case of the related ratio, Rumelt identified market or technological *links* between individual product-markets in constructing the ratio for respective firms. Therefore Rumelt provides a systematic analysis of synergy links between corporate activities for 246 large US corporations; as such it appears consistent with the framework developed earlier. However, while the single products and unrelated strategies are obviously polar opposites, it is perhaps not so clear where the other strategies fall in the spectrum of activity relatedness. Therefore we suggest an order of activity relatedness for the respective strategies by using Fig. 6.1 for illustrative purposes. Suppose we have

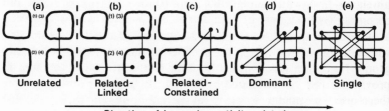

FIGURE 6.1   Activity relatedness of strategies

a firm split into four activities of equal revenue generating capacity. If there are links between activities we assume there are two possible ways this may occur: a market *or* technological link exists, in which case the activities are related; or market *and* technological links exist, in which case we have identical activities. Thus, in Fig. 6.1., a single link between two activities indicates they are related, while a double link indicates identical activities.

In case (a) two activities are related, but the related ratio is less than .7; therefore we have the case of the unrelated strategy. If activities (3) and (4) in case (a) also had a link with one other activity we would have the related-linked case as in case (b). However if our related group of activities in case (b) were to be linked as in the related-constrained strategy we would need stronger linking as in case (c) where *all* activities are linked one to another within the related group. Both (b) and (c) are related type strategies having related ratios of greater than .7 but the related-constrained strategy involves richer interconnections. As far as the dominant business category is concerned, the critical point for the ratio defining this category is also .7 as in the related type case, but in this case the relevant ratio is the *specialisation* ratio which requires both market and technological links between the activities composing the largest specific product-market; case (d) illustrates a dominant business strategy. The final strategy is the single business strategy, case (e), in which at least 95 per cent of the firm's activities are identical and case (e) is therefore illustrated as having both market and technological links between all four activities. In Fig. 6.1 activity relatedness, in terms of the extent of linking between activities, tends to increase from left to right; that is, activity relatedness increases in the order unrelated, related-linked, related-constrained, dominant, single. However, this simple progression should be regarded with some reservation; for example an unrelated firm with a single business contributing 69 per cent of corporate revenues may be regarded as being richer in links between activities (and therefore activity relatedness) than a related type firm with a related ratio of .7 and a variety of businesses within the related group. The specialisation and related ratios are measures which provide crude cut-off points for the respective strategies, and therefore the general ordering of strategies in terms of activity relatedness should be treated with caution.

For our purposes, an extremely valuable part of Rumelt's analysis distinguishes firms by strategy and industry. Rumelt found it possible to allocate even 'unrelated' strategies to industries in most cases; only 6 multi-industry firms were identified. This was achieved by allocating each firm to the industry that was the most representative of its major business activities.[3] Rumelt's primary concern in identifying firms by industry is in investigating possible relationships between financial performance and strategy. Here we are concerned with possible relationships between strategy and synergy/catastrophe effects. In order to do so, we use as indicator of technological progressiveness the mean level of company funds for R & D as a percentage of sales for each industry over the decade preceding 1969, the year in which the strategies were sampled. Table 6.1 is constructed from the corresponding table in Rumelt's analysis by rearranging the industries in order of technological progressiveness.

In the previous chapter we constructed Fig. 5.5 as a box diagram with activity relatedness increasing from left to right, and threat of catastrophe increasing in a vertical direction. Table 6.1 uses indicators that intendedly parallel the arrangement in Fig. 5.5 In fact we should expect to be able to overlay Fig. 5.5 on Table 6.1 and identify a trend towards increasing activity relatedness as environmental technological change diminishes. Is the information contained in Table 6.1 consistent with expectations?

We have identified two related trends in Table 6.1, i.e. (a) identifying for each industry the median strategy (measured along the activity relatedness dimension) and joining the median strategies for industries adjacent on the vertical dimension and (b) identifying for each strategy the median industry (measured along the technological change dimension) and joining the median strategies for strategies adjacent on the horizontal dimension. Trend (a) is indicated by a heavy line, trend (b) by a dotted line.

Trend (b) shows a distinct tendency for the median industry to become increasingly technologically stable as the level of activity

TABLE 6.1 Distribution of strategies in Rumelt's analysis for selected sample from Fortune 500 for 1969

Strategy / Industry	(2) Unrelated	(3) Related-Linked	(4) Related-contrained	(5) Dominant	(6) Single	(7) Company funds for R&D (% of sales, 1960-9)
Industrial chemicals	5	7	4	1		3.94
Instruments	2		1			3.89
Electrical	3	8	2		1	3.57
Aircraft and missiles	6		1	2		3.18
Machinery	4	4	8	7		3.05
Drugs and other chemicals		3	9	1		2.98
Transportation	3	5	2	4	1	2.49
Stone, clay and glass		4	1	1	1	1.63
Rubber			1	4		1.57
Fabricated metal products	1	1	1	2		1.20
Petroleum			2	7		0.97
Primary metals		1		7	1	0.74
Paper		1	1	7	1	0.73
Textiles and apparel		1	3			0.40
Lumber and furniture	1			2		0.40
Food	2	4	8	7	6	0.36

NOTE   Rumelt also identified one 'miscellaneous' and six 'multi-industry' firms.

SOURCES   Column (1) – (6) from Rumelt (1974) p.98.
Column (7) from National Science Foundation (1973, p.63).

relatedness associated with a specific strategy increases. This is consistent with the pattern predicted from Fig. 5.5 While trend (a) follows a more erratic path, it also appears to follow the rough trend which would be characteristic of a process of synergy/catastrophe threat trade-off. We can also break down the strategies into four basic groupings by distinguishing the R & D intensive industry groupings from the 8 lesser R & D intensive groupings, and also distinguishing single/dominant from related/unrelated strategies in Table 6.2. As we would expect, strategies tend to be clustered in the top left and bottom right boxes. A chi-square test indicated a value of 32.48 which is significant at the .005 level.

TABLE 6.2   Distribution of strategies in Rumelt's analysis by major groupings

Industry	Strategy	Related and unrelated	Single and dominant
Technologically progressive		82	19
Technologically unprogressive		28	44

Because of the more detailed information it contains, trend (a) is perhaps the more interesting of these three ways of classifying strategy in Table 6.1. One way of pursuing our analysis further is to consider why *exceptions* to the general trend exist. Why for example does trend (a) appear to break down in the bottom half of Table 6.1? In this case five industries have a dominant median strategy and three have a related-constrained median strategy; however shifts in median strategy do not appear to be influenced in the predicted direction by changes in technological progressiveness. The trend line 'kinks' up to the right for the low technology industries.

An interesting feature of the five dominant median strategy industries is that of the 27 actual dominant strategies in these cases, 25 are dominant-vertical strategies[4]; in fact these industries contained the bulk of the dominant-vertical firms, with only four of the other 24 dominant business firms falling into the dominant-vertical category[5], all four being in the extremely heterogenous food industry.

The most obvious reason for the perverse behaviour of the trend line in Table 6.1 is technological. As Rumelt points out; 'escape from these industries is particularly difficult for the large vertically integrated firm. Its technologies tend to be based on process rather than science or product function and are not readily transferable. Large size[6] implies that the scale of investment in new businesses must be large if noticeable changes in corporate performance are to be achieved, but low price-earnings ratios and high pay-out policies make such investments financially quite difficult.[7] Finally, the integrated businesses train few generalists, and their attitudes and the organisational structure they preside over tend to inhibit strategic change'. (Rumelt, 1974, p.139)

It can be argued that the advantages which make a vertically integrated strategy desirable in the first place may have the complementary disadvantage of locking corporations into a massive and inflexible commitment to a highly specialised capital intensive activity. As Rumelt (1974, pp.103-1) points out, these industries tend to be slow growing,[8] and consequently we might expect their low profitability, widespread overcapacity and unavoidable capital commitment to inhibit diversification in many cases. Also, even a moderate rate of technological change may add greatly to the capital demands associated with such strategies, further inhibiting diversification. In such cases, tactical considerations dominate, driving out the environmental signals that indicate the need for strategic change.

Thus we suggest that what appears as a kink in the general diagonal shift of trend (a) may be due to violation of a basic assumption, that a requisite degree of hedging is the prime objective of the firm. Pure synergy in the form of economies of scale appears to have been the objective of the firm in these cases. Even if technological economies of scale are exhausted, the management may perceive real or illusory diseconomies in diversifying into new, unfamiliar areas. Thus these vertically integrated industries emphasise synergy based on a specific material rather than attainment of an appropriate degree of hedging. Whether such deviance is rational due to exceptionally high opportunity cost of synergy sacrificed through hedging in these cases, or whether it is a consequence of tunnel-vision generated by historical dependence on a single material, we leave as an open question.

It may be possible to account for further exceptions to the trend. For example, the reasons for the existence of single or dominant strategies in the science-based industries may be dependent in a number of cases on high growth and profitability associated with the early stages of the product life cycle, as in the case of Xerox.[9] Again, these would be cases running counter to the assumptions of our model in so far as we assume product maturity and no barriers to entry to any specific strategy.

The PhD theses by Channon, and Dyas and Thanheiser provide rather less detailed information. In each case the sample is restricted to the 100 largest firms in Great Britain (1969–70), France (1970) and Germany (1970) respectively. This is understandable, since individual

TABLE 6.3   Strategies in science-based and non-science-based industries in three countries

	Single		Dominant		Related	
	S	N	S	N	S	N
(1) UK	1	5	3	31	26	28
(2) France	1	15	3	29	19	23
(3) Germany	4	18	4	18	24	13

S = firm in science-based industry
N = firm in non-science-based industry
SOURCES   Row (1) Channon (1973, pp.52–62).
          Row (2) Dyas and Thanheiser (1976, pp.269–79).
          Row (3) Dyas and Thanheiser (1976, pp.141–8).

European countries are rather less populated by large corporations than is the US. Further, while the major strategic categories were consistent with Rumelt's definitions in each case, none of the theses distinguishes between sub-categories of dominant or related strategies; thus we cannot distinguish between vertically integrated, related-constrained and related-linked strategies. Also none of the studies allocate unrelated strategies to industries.

In the light of the more restricted nature of available data compared to Rumelt's analysis, we summarise the available data into strategies for firms in science-based and non-science-based industries, as shown in Table 6.3. There is a close similarity in terms of the distribution of strategies in Britain, France and Germany. For each country science-based firms constituted less than 20 per cent of single business strategies and less than 20 per cent of dominant business strategies; however these firms constituted at least 45 per cent of all related strategies in each country. Thus, while the data in these cases is rather blunter than in Rumelt's analysis, it does illustrate rough trends consistent with that exposed in the US case.

Another associated topic of relevance here is the pattern of R & D diversification identified by Nelson, Peck and Kalachek (1967, pp.51–2). They calculated coefficients of specialisation (per cent of R & D expenditures by the firms in an industry directed towards that industry's major products). The results are indicated in Table 6.4. Since we hypothesise strategy will tend to involve a lower degree of activity relatedness as the level of environmental technological change

TABLE 6.4   Coefficients of specialisation for US R & D activities in 1960.

Industry	Specialisation
Aircraft and missiles	67.9
Chemicals	80.3
Electrical equipment and communication	48.7
Fabricated metal products	32.4
Food and kindred products	78.1
Machinery	51.4
Transportation	58.1
Petroleum refining and extraction	52.6
Primary metals	58.8
Professional and scientific instruments	32.0
Rubber products	33.9

SOURCE Nelson *et al.* (1967, p.51), computed from National Science Foundation (1963, pp.80–1).

increases, we may expect R & D activity as a tool of diversification strategy to behave in a similar fashion. As a first step in examining this hypothesis, the correlation coefficient between coefficient of specialisation and research intensity (R & D/Sales) in Table 6.4 was calculated. However the correlation coefficient was only 0.04 and is not statistically significant.

This apparently negative finding may conceal behaviour consistent with expectations. The low correlation coefficient may in fact co-exist with a strong tendency for the *relatedness* of corporate R & D to decrease with level of technological change. In particular, the science-based industries generally offer a much greater diversity of activity *within* industry boundaries than do non-science based industries which tend to be based on a particular material or substance (especially Stone, Clay, Glass, Petroleum, Primary metals, Paper and Lumber).[10]

This point can be simply demonstrated by comparing Electrical with Petroleum and Instruments with Rubber Products. The level of specialisation of R & D is similar in both pairs, but in each case the science-based industry offers a far greater scope for reduced R & D relatedness. It may also be pointed out here that the high coefficient of specialisation of Chemicals may be largely attributed to the breadth of the industry specification, ranging as it does from industrial chemicals to pharmaceuticals.

What verdict can be made on this issue? A hint may be taken from Scots law which provides the option of a verdict of Not Proven in addition to the usual ones of Innocent and Guilty. Not Proven may be interpreted as; 'the evidence indicates culpability, but is not sufficient to prove guilt beyond reasonable doubt'. Similarly the evidence here is not really solid enough to provide strong support of the framework developed here – but it is suggestive.

OTHER STUDIES OF DIVERSIFICATION AND INVENTIVE ACTIVITY

One of the most persistent hypotheses in the diversification literature is that diversification is directly related to the existence within science-based firms of a pool of scientific and technological manpower. A number of studies have investigated this hypothesis. In this section we argue against this hypothesis and provide an alternative explanation of studies that purport to demonstrate a significant relationship between diversification and technical employment.

An early study by Gort (1962) found a significant relationship between degree of diversification (measured as ratio of non-primary to total employment) and the ratio of scientists and engineers to other employees (hence T-ratio) for 111 US manufacturing firms when both variables are measured at industry level. Amey (1964) found that degree of diversification (measured as the ratio of net output other than principal products of industry group *to* net output of principal products by firms in that industry) was significantly related to the level of employment of scientific manpower for 25 major UK industries. Three recent studies have also confirmed this relationship. Firstly, Hassid (1975) found that degree of diversification (same measure as Amey's) for a sample of UK manufacturing industries was significantly related to the T-ratio. Gorecki (1975) found degree of diversification (same measure as Gort's) for 44 UK manufacturing industries was significantly related to the T-ratio. Finally, Wolf (1977) found degree of diversification (same measure as Amey's) was significantly related to the T-ratio for 95 US manufacturing industries.

In each case the diversification measure was positively and significantly related to the measure of scientific and technical employment. In each case the reason provided by the researcher was that the R & D skills internal to firms stimulated diversification activity.[11] Thus, the level of internally generated opportunities determine the extent of diversification in this view.[12] This contrasts with the interpretation put forward in the last chapter that the extent of diversification is determined by the potential level of externally generated threats.

There are three other studies which are of relevance here, but before they are introduced, a study by Mueller (1966) provides relevant information. Mueller found consistently high correlations between patents/R & D expenditure and patents/T-ratio for a number of major US manufacturing industries. According to Mueller there is a 'significant relationship between what goes into inventive process and what comes out of it' (p.36). He concludes that if used with care, patents, R & D expenditure and T-ratio may provide the researcher with satisfactory indices of inventive activity.

Thus we can interpret the T-ratio in each study above as a measure of the level of industrial inventive activity. We shall bear this in mind in looking at the next three studies by Scherer (1965), Grabowski (1968) and Comanor (1965). In each case they searched for possible relationships between diversification and inventive activity *within* specific industries. If we were to hold the 'technical skills' hypothesis, Mueller's findings suggest we would expect to find a significant relationship between diversification and inventive activity in each study.

Scherer (1965) found that a measure of diversification (measuring number of distinct product lines for the company) for 448 firms from the Fortune 500 for 1955 was strongly correlated with patenting intensity for the same firms in 1959 (r_2 of .37). However when the firms were allocated to 14 two-and three-digit industries and regression equations run for each industry with patenting intensity as dependent variable, and sales and degree of diversification as independent variables, the results were conflicting. For five industries the partial correlation coefficients between patenting intensity and diversification were *negative* but statistically insignificant (and this included the cases of the science-based electrical and general chemicals industries). For nine other industries (mostly non-science-based) the partial correlation coefficients were positive.

After a more detailed examination of the data and individual cases, Scherer concluded that the reason for the positive partial correlation coefficients was that the more diversified the firm in non-science-based industries, the higher the probability that it would also operate in a more progressive industry condusive to inventive activity. Thus, Scherer concludes, diversification *per se* is not directly linked to inventive activity, but instead acts as an indicator that the firm also operates in patent-rich environments.

Scherer was looking for a link running from diversification to inventive activity rather than the other way around, which explains the form of the regression equation and the four-year lag in patent measurement. Nonetheless, if the 'technical skills' argument holds water, we would still expect to find evidence of a direct positive relationship between diversification and inventive activity in Scherer's analysis.

Comanor's findings (1965) reinforce Scherer's. Comanor found that R & D productivity (measured by total new product sales in their first two years) was in fact *negatively* related with diversification for a sample of 57 US pharmaceutical manufacturers after allowing for firm size and R & D employment. Grabowski (1968) obtained rather different results; using firms' R & D expenditures for the period 1959–62 as dependent variable, and a measure of diversification (number of 5-digit industries operated in by the firm)[13] as one of the independent variables, Grabowski found significant and positive relationships between the variables in a regression run for 16 chemical firms and also in a regression run for 10 drug firms. However another regression equation run for 15 petroleum firms did not indicate any significant relationship.

Again, while the direction of causation is hypothesised to run in the opposite direction in both cases, there is no evidence for any relationship between diversification and inventive activity in Comanor's analysis although Grabowski's analysis is consistent with such a connection in the chemical and drugs case. However, if these three studies are considered together, their results contrast sharply with the consistent pattern suggested by the five other studies using R & D manpower measures.

From the standpoint of the 'technical skills' hypothesis, this is difficult to account for; if internal technical skills stimulate diversification, we would still expect to find inventive activity and diversification correlated when we compare firms within specific industries (Scherer, Comanor, Grabowski) as well as when we compare industries (Gort, Amey, Hassid, Gorecki, Wolf). However seen from the point of view of the argument of the previous chapter, reasons for the differences between the two studies become clearer. We can summarise the differences in the following equation:

$$D = f(\phi, I)$$

Where D is a measure of the degree of diversification for a specific firm, ϕ is a measure of the firm's level of inventive activity, and I is a measure of the level of inventive activity of the industry in which the firm operates.

The 'technical skills' hypothesis concentrates on the relation between D and ϕ. In this perspective, relations between inventive activity and diversification are anticipated at the level of the firm *and* at aggregated or industry levels. This is where we encounter the problem of inconsistent evidence.

However, our analysis predicts relations between D and I; we expect that diversification will increase with the level of technological change of the industry, due to the environmental threat of potential catastrophe. The five industry level studies are consistent with this expectation. The conflicting results of the intra-industry studies of Scherer, Comanor and Grabowski do not disturb this conclusion. While in practice intra-industry and intra-firm variables will certainly affect the degree of diversification, our analysis is concerned with the problem of synergy versus the *environment*, and the Scherer, Comanor and Grabowski studies may be regarded as investigating the lower level problem of whether or not firms in our industry 'fine-tune' their strategies in the context of their common environment. Intra-firm measures of inventive activity play no part in our analysis. However there is no reason why it could not be extended to cover both firm and industry level inventive activity as in the equation above.[14]

There is a variant of the 'technical skills' hypothesis put forward by Rumelt (1974) and based on argument by Chandler (1966) to explain why science based firms tend to be more highly diversified than non-science-based firms. Following Chandler, Rumelt suggests (p.133) that the science-based industries utilise knowledge and techniques that are not related to a single material, product or process (indeed this was an important part of our discussion in the previous section). The higher level of diversification observed in science-based industries is regarded as a consequence of the technologies associated with these industries being more easily *extended* into new applications. There are echoes here of Gort's earlier position that 'diversification paradoxically depends upon specialisation, except that the relevant form of specialisation is in technical skills rather than in the specific goods and services produced'. (1962, p.135).

The extensibility argument leads us to expect that science-based firms wishing to diversify could exploit synergy by pursuing technologically related strategies. On the other hand, a non-science-based firm wishing to diversify would be more likely to be forced into an unrelated strategy. Thus we would expect to find unrelated strategies mostly in the non-science-based industries.

In fact, if we examine Rumelt's own data as presented in Table 6.1, we find the opposite pattern. If we interpret the six most R & D intensive in that table as the science-based industries, 28 per cent of science-based firms adopted unrelated strategies (the percentage rises to 34 per cent for the five most R & D intensive industries). However, only 7 per cent of non-science-based firms adopted an unrelated strategy. The extensibility argument connot account for the popularity of the unrelated strategy in the science based industries, whether we gauge this popularity in relative or absolute terms.

A further point worth emphasising here is that even if there is limited technological extensibility (i.e. potential technological synergy), there may be possible market extensibility (i.e. potential market synergy). Examples of this potential source of synergy are the Rank Organisation in the UK and AMF in the US, both of which have diversified into a variety of technologies within the leisure and sports industry. Therefore lack of technological extensibility need not lead to an unrelated strategy.

The puzzle disappears when the unrelated strategy is viewed as hedging against environmental threat. Merger and take-over would be an obvious mechanism by which non-science-based firms could obtain the benefits of an unrelated strategy in the absence of extensible technology if they so desired. The evidence that the unrelated strategy tends to be more frequent in the science based industries suggests that it is preferred by many science based firms; hedging explains why.

PORTFOLIO THEORY OF DIVERSIFICATION

The portfolio theory approach discussed in the last chapter was developed by Markowitz (1952 and 1959). Adelman (1961), Smith and Schreiner (1969), and Weston (1970) have considered conglomerate diversification as a form of diversification providing the benefits of stability of returns consistent with the portfolio approach through the combination of independent or negatively correlated investments. Since conglomerate mergers involve unrelated activities, it would be expected to be more likely to provide these benefits than a synergy rich, strongly linked combination.

However, empirical studies tend not to support this hypothesis. In the UK Utton (1969) found that a sample of diversified firms did not appear to enjoy a significantly different level of variability of rate of return on capital employed and compared to undiversified firms in the same industry. Bond (1974) found no relation between level of diversification (based on industry count) and profit rate variability (standard deviation of rate of return on total invested capital) for 157 large US manufacturing firms for 1963–7, after separating out the effect of firm size on these variables.

Since these studies do not support the portfolio theory, an obvious conclusion would be that our criticisms of portfolio theory in Chapter 5 are reinforced. However, it is not quite as simple as this. What appears to have been ignored or overlooked by commentators in this area is that we would expect diversification to provide a more stable profits stream *even if such portfolio effects are not an objective of diversification.* From equation (2) in Chapter 5 we would expect that as long as there is not perfect correlation between businesses, diversification should reduce profit variability; even if diversification were to be undertaken for other purposes, a side-effect should be to stabilise profits. Seen in this light, Bond and Utton's negative results are surprising.

Our explanation of these negative results is based on the hedging motive of diversification. Diversification is the mechanism which permits firms to operate relatively securely in turbulent environments. Thus, even though diversification *reduces* risk at corporate level (of the type associated with the trend *AB* in Fig. 5.2), it is associated with *increased* vulnerability to and frequency of catastrophe at activity level (*BC* in Fig. 5.2). Thus reduced variability on the one hand is offset by increased variability on the other. We would expect that if we were to examine the *individual* activities of science-based firms, they would tend to be associated on average with more variable patterns of returns than would activities of non-science-based firms.

Therefore, the framework developed in Chapter 5 is also useful in this context in providing an explanation of the results of empirical analyses of portfolio theory.

We can also identify parallels between the managerial utility model of the last chapter, and recent analyses in the financial literature relating to conglomerate merger. A number of studies have queried the relevance of the early portfolio theory approach for conglomerate strategy; firstly, Alberts (1966) pointed out that corporate diversification designed to reduce overall riskiness should be redundant from the point of view of the shareholders. This is because shareholders can easily diversify their own financial holdings and obtain risk-spreading benefits from the spread of investments in their portfolio without the need for corporate diversification, and also because if financial portfolio diversification takes place then corporate diversification should have no further effect on prices and yields of shares; *portfolio* diversification should already have compensated for inherent diversification of individual activities and so corporate diversification should be unnecessary.

These points are developed by Levy and Sarnat (1970) who describe the portfolio theory approach as the 'uneasy case' for conglomerate merger. Levy and Sarnat demonstrate that conglomerate merger cannot provide economic advantages (which includes risk-speading) in a perfect capital market. Levy and Sarnat argue that market imperfections are necessary to make a case for conglomerate merger. They suggest that a case for conglomerate merger may be made if the possibility of 'gamblers' ruin' is recognised. This is the possibility that a critical level of loss for the company will lead to bankruptcy. Lintner (1971) also recognises the conglomerate advantage of reduction in lenders' risks of bankruptcy losses. Lewellen (1971) adds further analysis to the implications of 'gamblers'' ruin from the point of view of shareholders; the conglomerate merger should reduce the probability of default due to bankruptcy since loss-makers can be cross-subsidised, and since there are transaction costs associated with bankruptcy this should be of benefit to the shareholders – corresponding benefits should be received by corporate management in the form of lower costs of capital. Higgins and Schall (1975) show that the effect of conglomerate diversification depends on the nature and probability of the transaction costs of bankruptcy.

The risk of default is an obvious transaction cost to shareholders that may be reduced by conglomerate merger. However, it may be worth examining further the conditions in which 'gamblers'' ruin is likely to be a serious possibility for the firm. Suppose we consider first of all the effect of variability in returns in the absence of threat of catastrophe such that the conditions of multiperiod risk associated with Fig. 5.1 hold; that is a level of loss in any time period (Q) at point G which means the firm is faced with the prospect of defaulting on payments due to creditors. In those circumstances, if management and the capital market are convinced of the absence of potential catastrophe, then the expected future profitability of the firm could be used as a guarantee of future.

The real problem for the firm obtains if there is a threat of catastrophe. In those circumstances bankruptcy is a real possibility. Suppose a catastrophe appears as in point *B* in Fig. 5.2 and the trend line of profits becomes *C* in Fig. 5.1. In those circumstances the capital market would not have a sound basis for funding the firm's short-term losses. The present activity cannot be relied on as a future source of funds, while any replacement activity is liable to be a drain on funds in the immediate future, as well as being an uncertain long term prospect. While trend stability with a constant E (π_t) is a sound basis on which the capital market can fund short term losses, catastrophe destroys this comfortable relationship.

Therefore there is some similarity between recent developments in the financial literature and the approach developed here in that both recognise threat of default as a justification for conglomerate merger. Further, it is suggested here that the possibility of default can be linked directly to life cycle considerations in both perspectives. However, while these similarities exist, they should not be overstressed, since the argument in the present analysis is based on managerial considerations. Transaction costs of bankruptcy are liable to exist for both management and investors, *but* the transaction costs will differ for the respective groups.

CONCLUSION

In this chapter a number of studies have been examined from the point of view of the framework developed earlier. We have looked at the distribution of strategy by environment in Rumelt's (1974) analysis and two related studies. We concluded that, as expected, there was a broad tendency for propensity to adopt increasingly diversified strategies to increase with the level of industry technological change. This was explained by the tendency for firms to hedge in the face of potential environmental change. Relatively specialised, highly related, strategies tended to be associated with low technology industries. It was suggested that some exceptions to the general pattern might be explainable in terms of violation of the assumptions of the model. One such important group was the vertically integrated industries, and their deviant behaviour was explained in terms of the 'locking-in' effect of vertical integration.

It was also suggested that corporate R & D, in its role as one arm of diversification strategy, would tend to become increasingly unrelated as the level of industry R & D increased. The data was interpreted as weakly supporting this hypothesis.

Of perhaps greater relevance was the re-appraisal of a number of studies analysing the relationship between inventive activity and diversification. Those studies which investigated relationships between degree of diversification and inventive activity at industry level tended to find consistently strong and positive relations. However, studies carried out at firm level reported mixed and contradictory results. The significance of the results at industry level were accounted for in terms of the framework developed here, since we would expect such patterns to be exhibited at this level (as the analysis of Rumelt's data demonstrated earlier). The confusing messages recorded at the level of the firm was set aside as a separate problem. It was argued that hypotheses suggesting that diversification is based on internal technical skills of the firm, or extensible technology, do not cope as well as the approach developed here in accounting for observed behaviour.

Finally, it was suggested that negative findings of tests of portfolio theory applied to conglomerate diversification were in themselves puzzling; even if risk spreading was not a motive, conglomerate diversification should be expected to reduce profit variability anyway, *ceteris paribus*. It was suggested that the reason for this result was that a greater degree of variability at activity level due to catastrophe was associated with conglomerate operation and that conglomerates coped with this variability by hedging.

We have looked at a variety of aspects of diversification strategy in this chapter. In the next chapter we shall further extend the approach by looking at the possible relationship between technological change, aggregate concentration, and the post-war merger wave.

7 Aggregate Concentration and the Direction of Merger

In this chapter we re-orientate our analysis to consider a set of topics related to changes in corporate strategy. So far we have suggested that corporate strategy is determined by balancing synergy gains against hedging considerations; synergy is obtained from internal relationships, while hedging is designed to permit the firm to cope with its environmental threat. The argument of this chapter revolves around the point that if the environment becomes more threatening we would expect strategy changes to follow.

As far as the post-war period is concerned, a feature of particular relevance is a general increase in the rate of technological change. The implications of accelerating technological change will be discussed in the first section which deals with changes in corporate strategy. The findings of this section lead naturally to a consideration of changes in

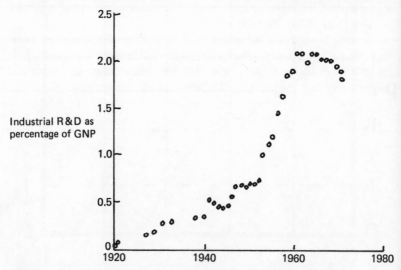

SOURCE   Clare (1963, p.137) and National Science Foundation (1973).
FIGURE 7.1   Performance of industrial research in the US

aggregate concentration in the second section. The third section discusses merger activity in US and UK industry and some conclusions are drawn as to the nature of recent merger activity of firms in a variety of industries. The fourth section considers a mixed bag of hypotheses and findings in the light of the preceding discussion.

CHANGES IN CORPORATE STRATEGY

Inventive activity in industry increased rapidly after the Second World War in the United States. Industrial R & D increased steadily from about 0.5 per cent of GNP in the late forties to over 2 per cent of GNP in the early sixties; see Clare (1963)), and National Science Foundation (1973). This trend is graphed in Fig. 7.1.

In the last chapter we argued that the level of inventive activity for an industry was a central determinant of the strategy of firms in that industry. Here we have a situation in which the overall level of industrial inventive activity increased rapidly in a relatively short

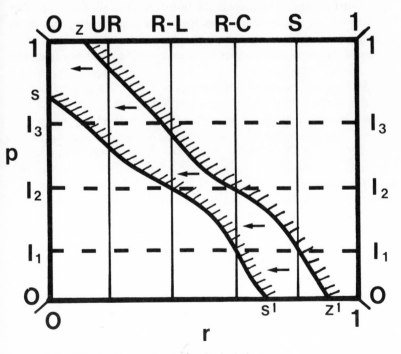

FIGURE 7.2   Effect of increasing technological change

period of time. We would expect this to have a substantial effect on individual corporate strategy and aggregate concentration. We shall deal first with the question of changing corporate strategy by reference to Fig. 7.2. This is based on Fig. 5.4, and as in that figure the survival constraint ZZ' slopes upwards from right to left. Now, suppose two conditions hold; the level of technological change increases for each industry, and each industry maintains its ranking relative to other industries[1]; how would we expect this to affect conditions facing the firm?

In those circumstances the survival constraint will shift to the left (SS' in Fig. 7.2). Each industry faces a *higher* level of technological change and consequently the required degree of hedging increases for all firms since environmental threat has increased in all sections. In Fig. 7.2 we have identified three sample industries; industry (1) on I_1I_1, industry (2) on I_2I_2 and industry (3) I_3I_3. In industry (1)'s case the utility maximising strategy shifts from single business to related-constrained, in industry (2)'s case the utility maximising strategy shifts from related-constrained to related-linked, in industry (3)'s case the utility maximising strategy shifts from related-linked to unrelated. Therefore in such circumstances we would expect highly synergistic (single business) strategies to be reduced in numbers while those strongly based on hedging (unrelated strategies) will become more popular. Intermediate strategies (here, related strategies) may increase or decrease depending on whether or not entry from formerly specialised strategies outnumbers exit to unrelated strategies.

The circumstances of post-war US industry development approximate to the conditions we assume above. While detailed industry data is patchy and irregular before 1957[2], from that date there is a regular pattern of growth in R & D activity for major sectors up to 1963,[3] while relative rankings by this measure tend to be maintained over this period.[4] Therefore, in this period we would expect to find the pattern of transformations in strategy described above. Table 7.1 describes the number of firms from Rumelt's sample in each strategic category for 1949, 1959, 1969, and provides some guide as to changes in strategy for the relevant period.

The pattern from 1949 to 1969 is as predicted, with a sharp decline in the number of single business strategies over the period, and the transformation of the unrelated strategy from a minor to a major strategy. However, another interesting feature is the rapid development of the related-linked strategy over this period. While such a pattern is consistent with more single/dominant/related-con-

TABLE 7.1 Distribution of strategies for large US firms
Estimated percentage of firms in each strategic category

Strategic category	1949	1959	1969
Single	34.5	16.2	6.2
Dominant-vertical	15.7	14.8	15.6
Dominant-constrained*	18.0	16.0	7.1
Dominant-linked*	0.9	3.8	5.6
Dominant-unrelated*	0.9	2.6	0.9
Related-constrained	18.8	29.1	21.6
Related-linked	7.9	10.9	23.6
Unrelated-passive	3.4	5.3	8.5
Acquisitive conglomerate†	0.0	1.2	10.9
Total firms	209	207	183

* The second term here refers to the direction of diversification outside the dominant product base.
† Unrelated firms pursuing an aggressive programme of acquisitions source over previous five years.
SOURCE Rumelt (1974, p.51), based on a selected sample from the Fortune 500 listings.

strained strategies feeding into the related-linked strategy than exit this category for the unrelated strategy, the growth in popularity of this strategy is in fact comparable with that of the unrelated or conglomerate strategy. The development of conglomerates has been well publicised, but Table 7.1 appears to indicate that it is paralleled by that of the related-linked strategy. This trend is distinctive enough to encourage suspicions that the related-linked strategy is more robust than might be suggested by its supposed role as a staging post for the unrelated strategy.

We can investigate this further by considering transition rates between categories for both decades. Table 7.2 indicates the percentage of firms in each category at the start of the decade that were still in the category by the end of the decade.[5] With minor exceptions firms that exited the strategy adopted a strategy with a higher associated degree of hedging. The results are interesting; as expected, the specialised strategies (single and most dominant categories) are characterised by high levels of emigration over the two decades, while proportionately few firms exit the two unrelated

TABLE 7.2   Strategic category transition rates, Fortune 500

| | Percentage of firms staying in each category | |
	1949–59	1959–69
Single	57.0	44.2
Dominant	75.2	70.3
Dominant-vertical	90.1	95.1
Dominant-constrained	51.6	43.9
Dominant-linked	50.0	50.0
Dominant-unrelated	100.0	16.7
Related	96.0	85.3
Related-constrained	94.3	58.5
Related-linked	100.0	81.9
Unrelated	100.0	100.0
Unrelated-passive	100.0	87.5
Acquisitive conglomerate	–	100.0

SOURCE   Rumelt (pp.56–7).

strategies over the same period. The related constrained strategy also appears to fulfil its role as a feeder for strategies with a higher degree of hedging; even though it increased its share of the Fortune 500 over the period (see Table 7.1) as a result of single and dominant business firms switching to this strategy, it still provides a rich source of related-linked and unrelated strategies over the two decades.[6]

However, there are two strategies which do not behave in accordance with simple expectations based on Fig. 7.2; firms operating dominant-vertical and related-linked strategies appear to be reluctant to switch to any other strategies over the two decades, despite apparently strong pressures to do so.

In the case of the dominant-vertical strategy, this is as we would expect from the evidence and argument of the last chapter. The vertically integrated firms tend to be locked into their strategies and typically experience difficulty in escaping from their restricted activities even in the face of increasing environmental threat.

Reasons for the resilience of the related-linked strategy are less obvious. We can begin to develop a suggested explanation by referring back to Fig. 4.10. Figure 4.10(b) indicates the direct nature of catastrophe linking in that it demonstrates how a single constituent shared by all activities can open up the firm to simultaneous attack on all fronts. However, suppose the *extent* of all shared constituents is limited; how might that affect synergy and hedging considerations?

Restriction on the sharing of constituents may in fact permit the related-linked strategy to obtain substantial hedging benefits. We can illustrate this by reference to the related-linked strategy in Fig. 6.1. Suppose activity (4) in this case faced the threat of catastrophe, but the shared constituent between (3) and (4) was not the constituent directly affected. In this case there would be no catastrophe linking. Activity (3) will be indirectly affected by the activity linking of the shared constituent X between (3) and (4), while activity (2) will also be affected by combined activity linking of the shared constituents X and Y.

We would expect catastrophe linking to be a stronger and more direct threat to survival than activity linking, and in this example catastrophe linking would have a maximum potential range of only two activities. Therefore, for a many-activity firm, the related-linked strategy should provide effective hedging for even highly turbulent environments, providing links are restricted to short ranges over activities. Catastrophe linking would be a localised problem, while the short range of links would also rapidly dampen the effects of activity linking. On the other hand, a single shared constituent in the related-constrained strategy could lead to possibly fatal consequences.

Therefore, the related-linked strategy has hedging potential approaching that of the unrelated strategy, and consequently may provide a genuine alternative to the unrelated strategy in even the most hostile environments.[7]

Seen in this perspective, the strategies in Table 7.3 fall into two distinct categories; the transitory and the 'sticky'. Dominant-vertical, related-linked, and unrelated all belong to the latter category for the reasons discussed above, and the pattern of strategy transformations in Table 7.3 is more comprehensible as a result.

CHANGES IN AGGREGATE CONCENTRATION

The analysis of the previous section has implications for the composition of large firms in the economy. The simplified exposition in Fig. 7.2 suggests a whole set of strategy transformations as a result of the shift in the survival constraint; single into related-constrained, related-constrained into related-linked, related-linked into unrelated. While we have qualified the last possible transformation, we would still expect to find a general switch to strategies with lower overall level of activity relatedness.

This should have an effect on aggregate concentration, or the relative importance of large firms in the economy. Before we consider more fully why this should be, it is useful to consider the relevance of aggregate concentration in neoclassical theory:

> In conventional economics the level of aggregate concentration has little meaning, as the theory is mainly concerned with economic power arising from operating in a single market. The power of a firm is no more than the sum of the power it exercises in each market in which it operates. (Aaronovitch and Sawyer, 1975, p.116)

This is as we would expect from our earlier criticism of neoclassical theory. In the context of the approach developed here, aggregate concentration is a misleading term; more accurately it should be interpreted as overall concentration, or large firms' share of industrial activity.

We can demonstrate the implications of our approach by considering how the firms may adapt their strategies when under pressure to do so as a result of a shift in the survival constraint in Fig. 7.2.

We start by stating two general principles: (a) combination of firms with like strategies cannot reduce the level of hedging and will generally increase it (b) combination of unlike strategies will increase the level of hedging relative to the strategy with the higher degree of activity relatedness.

The point of this rather clumsy looking pair of principles is that combination of firms favours hedging, not synergy. We can illustrate this by reference to Fig. 6.1. In each case, we could construct a specific strategy by combining appropriate firms from particular categories, or mix of categories, to the *right* of our desired strategy. For example, in Fig. 3.6 we combine three single businesses to obtain an unrelated strategy (firm Omega), while both firm Alpha and Beta may be regarded as the consequence of combining a single business (C and C' respectively) with a related-constrained strategy ($A + B$ and $A' + B'$ respectively). The first example is consistent with principle (a) and the second two with principle (b). The overall level of hedging increases in each case.

The reverse does not apply. We cannot combine like strategies and reduce the overall level of hedging. This means that we cannot obtain any strategy in Fig. 6.1 by any combination of firms operating strategies to the *left* of our desired strategy on the relatedness spectrum.

Now, suppose we have a rapid development in the rate of technological change as in the early post-war period in the US In this situation the firm will typically be faced with the necessity of rapidly increasing its level of hedging in a relatively short period of time. There are a number of options open to it for this purpose. For example, it could develop the new strategy through internal expansion. However, such a strategy would require time to develop, and since the object of the strategy is hedging there would be only slight links between old and new activities; consequently existing management will be unfamiliar with the new activities. Internal expansion of activities requires *time*, especially if hedging is the objective. For the period with which we are concerned, time is an extremely scarce resource.

Another strategy would maintain the size of the firm and increase hedging by divesting some activities with highly synergistic internal connections in exchange for more loosely related activities. However activity linking will inhibit divestment. Once synergy is being extracted there will be strong reluctance to sacrifice it.

In this case, objections to sacrificing synergy may be reinforced by the existence of a simple and obvious alternative that does not involve divestment. As is obvious from the discussion at the start of this section *merger* may provide requisite hedging. To the extent that mergers pursue hedging objectives, time is not likely to be an issue; in the limit, a totally unrelated strategy can be created literally overnight.

We can provide an example built around the illustrative cases of Chapter 3 as described in Fig. 3.6. We assume to start with that our survival constraint is ZZ' in Fig. 7.2 and that a rapid acceleration of technological change shifts the survival constraint to the left to SS'.

Suppose our original strategy is that of the aluminium ski firm. The shift in the survival constraint signals a switch to a related constrained strategy is desirable. Such a strategy can be achieved by merger, and in Fig. 3.6 the pairing of A' and B' would provide such a strategy. The resulting firm (Beta *less* C') operates a related-constrained strategy built around technological links.

However, suppose instead that this firm $(A' + B')$ was one of the

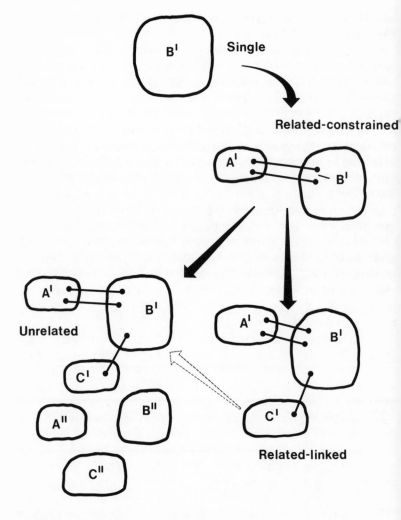

FIGURE 7.3 Development of strategy

original strategies operating on ZZ'. In those circumstances the shift in the survival constraint encourages adoption of a related-linked strategy. One way such a strategy could be achieved is by merging C' with A' and B' as in Fig. 7.3. The resulting firm Beta operates a related-linked strategy built around separate technological and market links.

If, instead, firm Beta was one of the original strategies on ZZ', we could construct an unrelated strategy by merging Beta and Omega. We describe this transition as a dotted line in Fig. 7.3 since we argued in the previous section that the related-linked strategy represents a genuine alternative mode of development for firms, and should not be merely regarded as source material for the unrelated strategy. The heavy line between the related-constrained and the unrelated strategy suggests the more likely line of development of unrelated strategies.

What each of these developments have in common is that the shift in the survival constraint stimulates the creation of *larger* firms. Hedging by merger increases the absolute size of firms, and this holds for all categories of firms whether they operate in low or high technology.

Thus, acceleration of technological change favours the development of large firms. We have argued the increased importance of large firms in absolute terms but we should expect the *relative* importance of large firms to increase also. The increasing rate of inventive activity charted in Fig. 7.1 should be paralleled by an increase in aggregate (overall) concentration.

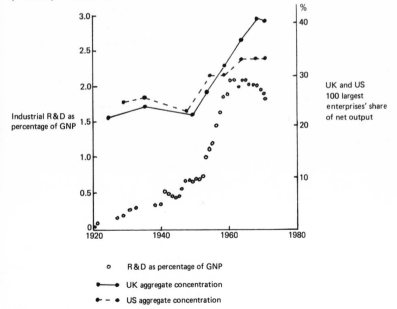

SOURCE Clare (1963, p.137), National Science Foundation (1973) and Prais (1976, p.140).

FIGURE 7.4 Changes in overall concentration and performance of industrial research in the US

As far as the trend in overall concentration in the UK is concerned the rise in the hundred largest firms share of net output is even more dramatic. There is little doubt that the increasing significance of technological change in the US over the post-war period is paralleled by the experience of UK industry. Even if there were *no* changes in the level of inventive activity in the UK, the US's role in providing a major leading edge in accelerating inventive activity over this period should have stimulated hedging by UK firms; environmental hostility is an international phenomenon, and is not restricted to domestic boundaries.

One interesting feature in Fig. 7.4 is the continuing trend towards increased concentration in the UK after 1963 in contrast to the constancy displayed by the US case. It may reflect differences in the growth and impact of inventive activity in the respective countries, or it may be the consequence of a lag effect in adjustment of UK firms compared to more progressive US firms (since hedging encourages large *absolute* size this might also explain the UK trend overtaking the US trend.) Alternatively, a number of commentators attribute the slowing up of the trend in the US to the increasing effectiveness of application of anti-trust law (Prais, 1976, pp.141 and 282–3; Scherer, 1970, pp.109–11, 489–90; Blair, 1972, Chapter 22). Scherer (1970, p.490) raises the possibility that strong prohibitions on horizontal mergers redirected managers' attentions to conglomerate mergers. Mueller (1969, pp.657–8) similarly suggests that the anti-trust squeeze on mergers switched managerial activity to the conglomerate area.

These studies invite comment. Firstly, the simultaneous levelling off of inventive activity and overall concentration in the US case may turn out to be coincidental; if, as would be reasonable to suppose, there is a lag effect in shifts in concentration relative to shifts in the level of inventive activity, then increase in concentration due to transitions in strategy may have been choked off by anti-trust policy before firms had achieved their desired strategy. Secondly, while Mueller's growth maximisation hypothesis is consistent with the approach developed here, it does not explain why conglomerate merger is apparently associated with some environments rather than others; nor does observation of changes in application of anti-trust policy explain this.

A further point suggested by these studies, and the earlier analysis of this section, is that merger is an extremely important mechanism underlying changes in overall concentration for the post-war period. If this is indeed the case, we should expect that our approach should be of some use in analysing merger activity, and possibly even changes in industry concentration, over the same period. We investigate this possibility in the next section.

INDUSTRY CONCENTRATION AND MERGER ACTIVITY

The first point we shall deal with here is the result of a finding by Aaronovitch and Sawyer (1975) that there did not appear to be any close relationship between merger activity and indicators of technical change for 13 major UK industries in the 1960s. Merger activity was measured in terms of the ratio AA/NA (assets acquired/net assets) for a given period, and inventive activity was measured both in terms of R & D as a percentage of sales in 1962, and qualified scientific manpower (QSM) as a percentage of total manpower in 1966. The Spearman rank correlation coefficient between the QSM measure and the AA/NA measure for 1955–68 was -0.165 and was not significant at the 0.05 level. The same correlation measure between the R & D measure and AA/NA for 1961–2, 1964–5 and 1966–7 was -0.1, 0.05, and 0.73 respectively. Aaronovitch and Sawyer draw the obvious conclusion that there appears to be no systematic relationship between merger activity and measures of inventive activity observed on an industry basis. On the other hand, Gort (1962) found a positive correlation between the number of product additions for industries entered and the T-ratio for three periods 1929–39, 1939–5 and 1950–5. Diversification activity and inventive activity appear to be strongly related in this case. A later study by Gort (1969) found that regression equations containing measures of industry concentration, growth and *two* measures of technological change (the T-ratio and proportionate change in labour productivity for the appropriate period) provided good explanations of merger rates for 46 US manufacturing industries (aggregate number of mergers *over* number of firms in industry in 1954 with assets over \$500,000) for 1951–9.

There may be a single explanation for the contradictory results between Aaronovitch and Sawyer's results and Gort's results. As was explained in the last section, a general shift in the level of technological change would create a general tendency to merge. This effect would be across the board, and not restricted to science-based firms. Whether or not technologically progressive firms merge more rapidly than non-science-based firms depends not on *speed* of technological change but on *acceleration*. If all industries grow from a low base of inventive activity, we would expect a positive correlation between *rate* and *acceleration* of technological change which might explain Gort's results. We do not have sufficient information to judge Aaronovitch and Sawyer's findings.[8]

The motivation to merge is stimulated by *changes* in the level of inventive activity not the level of inventive activity itself. However, we would expect the *direction* of merger to be determined by the actual level of inventive activity, the higher the degree of hedging associated with the desired strategy. For example, single business firms in low technology industries might shift to a related-constrained strategy with strong synergy links, while science-based firms might simply extend their unrelated strategy based around absence of synergy links. In Fig. 7.2 we would expect the degree of synergy sought by merger to diminish as we move up the new survival constraint.

If we approach this problem with caution we should be able to consider changes in level of industry concentration for a situation comparable to that described in Fig. 7.2. If we identify fairly broad industry categories then we would expect the likelihood of intra-industry merger to diminish as the level of inventive activity increases; synergy-conscious low technology firms are more likely to stay within their own industry boundaries than hedging-conscious science-based firms. If inventive activity is increasing for a science-based industry, we would expect to find firms in the industry hedging by merging *out* of the industry, while firms in other science-based industries with rising levels of inventive activity may hedge by merging *with* this industry. Caution is advised in this respect because the broadness of the industry category is crucial. For the broadest categories, at 2-digit level, most strategies may well be achieved within industry boundaries. For the narrowest categories, say 4- or 5-digit level, almost all firms may have to move out of existing areas for merger purposes. It is at intermediate levels, around 3- or 4-digit level, that we may expect to find the connection between concentration changes and inventive activity.

The connection we would expect is that for moderately broad industry categories, the situation outlined in Fig. 7.2 will be more favourable to increases in industry concentration in the low-technology industries than in the science-based industries. In the science-based industries, the combination of external merger by existing firms and entry by other science-based firms will make concentration increases less likely.

A study by Blair (1972) conveniently summarises concentration for a number of industries around this level. Blair selected major US

manufacturing industries with a value of shipments of over $1 billion
whose concentration ratios changed by more than 3 percentage points
between 1947 and 1967. The concentration ratio measured the percentage of value of shipments controlled by the four largest firms in each
industry. There were 48 industries in Blair's sample.

In Fig. 7.1, inventive activity increased steadily from the late forties
to early sixties, and accordingly we shall consider changes in concentration from 1947 to 1963. In Table 7.3, we allocate these industries to
the 2- or 3-digit industries for which NSF data on inventive activity
is available. Inventive activity is measured at the narrowest possible
industry category and the indicator used is R & D as a percentage of
sales for 1960; this year was the first for which NSF was available at
least at 2-digit level for all industries. Table 7.3 is arranged in
descending level of R & D intensiveness. One industry (steel foundries)
reported no change in level of concentration. The results are very
interesting. If we identify a cutoff point between Petroleum and

TABLE 7.3   Inventive activity and change in industry concentration

	(1) R & D funds as % of net sales	(2) Increase in concentration 1947–63	(3) Decrease in concentration 1947–63
Aircraft and missiles	23.2	–	1
Industrial chemicals	5.7	–	2
Optical and other instruments	5.3	1	–
Machinery	4.7	–	2
Drugs	4.6	–	1
Transportation	3.0	1	1
Other chemicals	2.2	1	–
Stone, clay and glass	1.6	–	1
Fabricated metals	1.3	–	4
Petroleum	1.0	–	1
Ferrous	0.6	2	–
Lumber	0.6	1	–
Textiles	0.6	8	1
Food	0.3	6	4

SOURCES   Column (1) National Science Foundation (1973, p.61).
Columns (2), (3) Blair (1972, pp.20–2).

Ferrous, then only 19 per cent of the R & D intensive industries report an increase in concentration over the period 1947–63, while 81 per cent of these industries report a decrease. On the other hand, 77 per cent of the less-R & D-intensive report an increase in concentration while only 23 per cent report a decrease.

However this result should be qualified by the observation that the 5 'other manufacturing' industries in Blair's sample all reported decreases; two tobacco industries, newspapers, periodicals and games and toys. Since this was a catch-all category it was excluded from Table 7.3. However, if separate R & D figures were obtainable, it is likely they would all fall into the lesser-intensive category in this case. Nevertheless the results are broadly consistent with expectations and tends to further reinforce faith in the approach developed here.

It would be useful if we had data on merger activity at 3- and 4-digit level for the early post-war period to set against changes in industry concentration. These are not available, but a study by Wood (1971) provides merger data at the 2-digit level for the appropriate period. The study analysed mergers by the 100 most acquisitive firms for 1950–63.[9] The results are shown in Table 7.4.

The ratio of mergers internal to the home industry (I) to all mergers (T) was calculated, and is set out in Table 7.5 along with a measure of inventive activity (R & D as a percentage of sales for 1960). The correlation coefficient between I/T and R & D/sales is -0.31. This is in the direction predicted, but is not statistically significant even at the 90 per cent level of significance.

However, this exercise might still be useful even though the 2-digit level is really too broad for our purposes. The five most R & D intensive industries all report I/T ratios below the mean level, as we would expect, with one exception; chemicals. Chemicals has a high I/T ratio and a high R & D/sales ratio. Yet as Blair (1972) comments for roughly the same period (1947–67):

> Among industry groups characterised by generally declining concentration, the most conspicuous was chemicals and allied products. In the group as a whole decreases well outnumbered increases, and 3 of the chemical industries in which concentration fell had shipments of more than \$1 billion. (p.21).

The industries which Blair mentions are indicated in the two chemical industry categories in Table 7.3. However, in addition Blair confirms that the typical pattern in the chemical industry is one of declining

TABLE 7.4   Mergers by the 100 most acquisitive manufacturing firms, 1950–63: assets ($ million)

Industry of product \ Industry of firm	Food (10 firms)	Tobacco (1)	Textiles (3)	Paper, etc. (14)	Chemicals (13)	Petroleum (11)	Rubber (3)	Stone, clay, glass (3)	Primary metals (8)	Fabricated metal products (3)	Machinery (8)	Electrical machinery (6)	Transport equipment (15)
Food	735				75								
Tobacco													
Textile products and apparel	60		703				13						
Wood, paper, printing		13		2056	80				75	3	498	13	
Chemicals	108	3		28	1425	550	13	3		60	280	3	33
Petroleum					153	1280							
Rubber							63						
Stone, clay, glass				5	80		180	13				3	390
Primary metals	73				78		60	3	365				75
Fabricated metal products	3								15		75	75	45
Non-electrical Machinery				15			13				346	118	353
Electrical machinery									75		83	493	483
Transportation equipment	13					150	73	73				3	1026
Instruments	3			60		3				3	5	370	15
Total	995	16	703	2164	1891	1983	235	161	471	561	875	1065	2420

Grand total: $13 540 million

SOURCE   Wood (1971, p.438).

concentration even though chemical industry as a whole tended not to diversify outside its own boundaries.

We can use this information to make inferences about probable strategies in both the industrial chemicals and drugs plus other chemicals industries. Industrial chemicals being highly research intensive, but apparently reluctant to diversify out of the 2-digit industry, we would expect it to have chosen the related-linked method of hedging rather than the unrelated strategy. On the other hand, drugs plus other chemicals constitutes the median category for both

TABLE 7.5   External and internal mergers at 2-digit industry level, and inventive activity

	I/T	R & D/sales
Food	74	0.4
Textiles	100	0.6
Paper, etc.	95	0.7
Chemicals	75	4.5
Petroleum	65	1.0
Rubber	27	2.0
Stone, clay and glass	69	1.6
Primary metals	77	0.8
Fabricated metals	0	1.3
Machinery	40	4.7
Electrical machinery	46	11.2
Transportation	42	3.0

SOURCES   *I/T* ratio from Wood (1971) p.438.
R & D/sales ratio from National Science Foundation (1973, p.61).

related strategies on trend line (b). We would expect to find evidence of a preference for a related-linked strategy in the industrial chemicals case and related-linked *or* related-constrained in the drugs case. The broadness of the chemical industry boundaries would allow fulfilment of these strategies within the industry itself, and would be consistent with a high I/T ratio.

Table 6.1 does indicate that 41 per cent of firms in the industrial chemicals case for Rumelt's sample pursued a related-linked strategy, while 92 per cent in the drugs plus other chemicals case pursued a related strategy. Together with the other data, this paints a picture of chemical industry (and other) firms diversifying into other chemical industries; the combined effect of neglecting to extend their existing activities and of entering other chemical industries is to lower concentration.[10]

Thus there are grounds for believing that we can usefully combine analysis of merger activity, changes in industry concentration, and corporate strategy if we are careful in our identification of the level to which our analysis applies. As far as 2-digit analysis is concerned, we make the same point with respect to the overly broad industry categories that was made in discussion of R & D diversification earlier. Comparable patterns hold: here chemicals has a similar *I/T* ratio to the food industry even though the food industry performs one basic function, while the chemical industry is multifunction; similarly, even though petroleums records a 10 per cent lower I/T ratio than chemicals, this misrepresents a much more specialised strategy on the part of petroleum firms since petroleum is based on one basic material, while chemicals is based on numerous substances and materials. To complicate matters even further, the non-chemical science based firms (aircraft and missiles, instruments, electrical equipment and machinery) could well pursue related strategies by *inter*-industry merger among themselves in a number of cases.

We have more evidence to justify reservations with respect to 2-digit industry analysis than was available for the R & D diversification analysis, and to that extent our earlier criticism is reinforced. The value of looking at 2-digit level in this section has been in an informal look at the internal consistency of our approach in considering a variety of problems related to strategy, aggregate concentration, industrial concentration, merger activity and diversification. Our approach is resilient in being able to explain difficulties at 2-digit level. Formal testing of hypotheses relating to merger activity in a period of increasing technological change require more precise information on diversification links for narrower industry categories. However our approach again permits us to suggest an explanation of apparently inconsistent results mentioned at the start of this section with respect to possible relationships between inventive activity and merger activity; Gort found a positive relationship between the T-ratio and merger activity and changes in labour productivity and merger activity for 1951–9 in the US. The first measure may stand as a proxy for rate of *acceleration* of technological change in the 1950s in the US, while the second may provide a more direct measure of this variable. On the other hand, Aaronovitch and Sawyer conducted their analysis in the decelerating 1960s in which the direct connection between acceleration and speed of technological change may no longer be necessarily expected. Further, the historic US role as a leader in technological change means that it can be more reasonably treated in isolation over this period, while UK diversification is more likely to be affected by foreign technological change, and consequently domestic inventive activity may be a weaker indication of external threat.

SUMMARY

The last chapter concentrated on aspects of corporate strategy at a particular point in time. In this chapter we have considered changes in corporate strategy over time. Our approach leads us to expect that there would have been a general switch towards strategies associated with a higher degree of hedging in the post-war period, and the evidence of the first section is consistent with this.

Increases in overall concentration are also predicted as a result of accelerating technological change, and section two suggests that this has been the case in the post-war period. The post-war merger wave is also explainable in this context as a drive towards increased hedging as protection against technological change.

Changes in industry concentration for moderately broad industry categories were also consistent with expectations, though more difficulty was experienced in making sense of merger activity at 2-digit level due to the broadness of the industry categories. However, previous studies of merger activity for narrower industry categories were consistent with the prediction that merger activity was a consequence of the *acceleration* of technological change, not the *level* of technological change.

Thus this chapter and the preceding chapter have provided a fairly comprehensive analysis of corporate strategy and strategic changes in the post-war period. We have concentrated on the early post-war period partly because of availability of data and existing studies for this period, but also because the conditions of that period make it easier to identify likely trends. The later post-war period is more erratic as far as trends in the level and rate of change of inventive activity is concerned.

This chapter and the preceding chapter have covered a broad territory comprising corporate strategy, changes in strategy, degree of industry diversification, changes in overall and industry concentration, and merger activity. The framework developed earlier has merit in being able to construct a coherent interpretation of these topics and their relationship to one another.

8 Strategy and Structure

This chapter provides the opportunity to outline an integrated framework for the analysis of corporate strategy and internal organisation (or structure). Chandler's historical analysis (1966) of the development of the multi-divisional corporation suggests that structure tends to follow strategy, for the reasons discussed in Chapter 4. Williamson's analyses (1970 and 1975) develop further the reasons for structures dependency on strategy, while Ansoff (1965, pp.144–7) argues in a normative context that structure should follow synergy. These studies all suggest that an integration of strategy and structure considerations should be possible. Our analysis of strategy and internal organisation in Chapter 4 may be regarded as providing further support for this viewpoint; internal organisation was identified as a function of *internal* transaction costs, which was in turn dependent on the synergy content of strategy.

We shall argue in this chapter that this position is correct as far as it goes, but that it is incomplete. Firstly, these studies look only at one dimension of internal organisation, though it has been well established that there exists another important dimension. Secondly, once we recognise both this new dimension and the implications of catastrophe, then strategy and structure are both seen as being dependent on environmental technological change. We shall return to the second point later in the chapter, but to start with we shall consider the dimensions of internal organisation.

DIMENSIONS OF INTERNAL ORGANISATION

We shall identify two main dimensions of internal organisation. The first is associated with the polar types of M-form and U-form structures, and is dependent on corporate strategy. The second is associated with the polar types of mechanistic and organic structures, and is dependent on degree of environmental technological change.

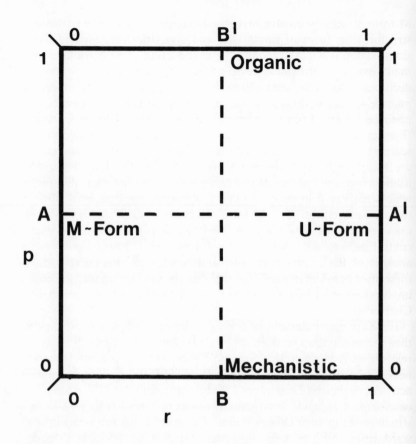

FIGURE 8.1   Structure

(a) *The Activity Relatedness Dimension*

This dimension has been well discussed in Chapter 4. Williamson (1970, 1975) has argued that the M-form structure has superior strategy formulating and internal control properties to the U-form; 'the organisation and operation of the large enterprise along the lines of the M-form favors goal pursuit and least cost behaviour more nearly associated with the neoclassical profit maximisation hypothesis than does the U-form organizational alternative'. (1975, p.150)

The relevant strategy formulating and internal control advantages of the M-form *vis à vis* the U-form were discussed in Chapter 4. What Williamson omits in this context is recognition of the probability that

M-form structures involve higher managerial costs than do U-form structures for firms of similar size and diversification. Firstly, divisionalisation is liable to require the introduction of an *extra* layer of management at divisional level to intercept and act on strategic decisions. Secondly, the divisional managers must be general managers, that is they must be capable of running a section comprising a variety of functions such as manufacturing, sales, R & D and finance; skilled or even competent general managers are liable to be scarcer than the most specialised functional managers they replace and are therefore liable to be more expensive. Thirdly, full divisionalisation requires full functional representation within each division, which may result in expensive and unnecessary duplication of functional management. The M-form structure is likely to have these managerial costs to set against its strategic overview and internal control advantages when compared with the U-form. For a full analysis of the comparative costs and benefits of alternative forms these must be taken into account, as must the *internal* transaction cost implications of M-form and U-form alternatives as discussed in Chapter 4.

If we are manipulating one variable, degree of activity relatedness, then the relationship between organisation form and degree of activity relatedness is fairly straightforward for extremes of activity relatedness. Following the transaction cost analysis of Chapter 4, high activity relatedness encourages U-form structure (as in firm Alpha's case, Fig. 4.3) while low activity relatedness encourages M-form structure (as in firm Omega's case, Fig. 4.4). These are straightforward cases, but we have suggested there is an M-form/U-form *dimension*. How do we deal with intermediate cases?

The interpretation of the concept of dimension is illustrated in Fig. 4.5 and 4.6 respectively (firms Chi and Pi respectively). Both cases may be interpreted as mixed forms with features of both M- and U-form structures. In both cases rich synergy links result in a separate function reporting directly to general office, while absence or weakness of links in other functions encourages divisionalisation for both firms. Again, links between activities encourage functional grouping, absence of links encourages divisional grouping. The principle of grouping richly connected areas of decision-making still applies for intermediate forms. Therefore we would expect that movement along the activity relatedness dimension from A' to A in Fig. 8.1 would be parallel by a shift from an organisation form in which U-form characteristics strongly dominate to one in which M-form characteristics strongly dominate. We hypothesise the transition from U-form to M-form is gradual with the proportion of groupings by activity rather than function increasing as we move from A' to A. Strategic and control considerations may encourage all-or-nothing divisionalisation in some cases but we would still expect to find the general pattern of organisation forms to be closely dependent on strategy in the manner suggested here.

(b) *The Technological Change Dimension*

This second dimension has been closely analysed by organisation theoriests though not economists. An early work by Burns and Stalker (1961) set the context for subsequent analysis on the relationship of organisation form to environmental technological change. While there has been continuing interest in this problem by organisation theorists, it has been largely ignored by economists.

Burns and Stalker identified two polar forms of organisation form, mechanistic and organic. The mechanistic form is appropriate to stable conditions in which technology is changing slowly. It is characterised by a well-defined hierarchic structure of control, authority and communication in which individuals specialise in precisely stated tasks according to the directions of superiors (Burns and Stalker, 1961, p.120). The organic form is appropriate to unstable conditions in which technology is changing rapidly and problems cannot be automatically anticipated and dealt with routinely. It is characterised by a network structure of control, authority and communication in which communication tends to be in the form of lateral consultation and advice rather than vertical orders and instructions, and there is continual re-definition of tasks and relationships as internal and external conditions change (Burns and Stalker, 1961, p.121). Organic systems are not hierarchic in a similar fashion to mechanistic systems, but are stratified according to seniority. Authority and responsibility is *ad hoc* and localised, not centralised.

In short, mechanistic systems tend to be characterised by rigid and formalised structure and behaviour, while organic systems tend to be characterised by flexibility and devolved responsibilities. Burns and Stalker state explicitly that they regard the two forms as a polarity, not a dichotomy; intermediate stages may exist depending on circumstances.

From an economic perspective these structures are extremely interesting in that they are naturally explicable in control-loss terms. We can provide a simple example to support this argument. Suppose we have a firm operating in a technologically stable environment. In those circumstances most decisions are routine, repetitive and follow well defined patterns. As a consequence, individual roles and responsibilities can be precisely ordered and set at all levels within a mechanistic system. The environment rarely throws up unexpected change, and when it does it the element of surprise can ensure that it is quickly referred upwards to senior levels for strategic decision.[1] Now, suppose we progressively increase the level of environmental technological change while holding corporate strategy and organisation constant. In such circumstances the level of non-routine, unprogrammed problems also increases. Even for relatively minor decisions there is less likelihood that it will follow established patterns. This results in referral upwards of an increasing proportion of problems for clarification and an increasing proportion of proposals for sanctioning by higher management. The individual at lower levels does not have the authority to act independently when new problems arise; the alternative to referral upwards is to ignore the problem and act according to rules and standard procedures, which may be even more disastrous for the organisation.

In such cases the organisation will be affected by decision delay, control loss and decision capacity bottlenecks at top level, just as the U-form organisation experiences as diversification increases. The gains from specialisation and division of labour provided by the mechanistic system dwindle as the level of environmental technological change increases, since these gains depend upon predictability of individual tasks; at the same time the decision costs of the mechanistic system increase. While the organic system does not provide the specialisation and division of labour gains of the mechanistic system, such gains cannot be exploited in rapidly changing environments in any case. On the other hand, the organic system cuts down on decision delay, control loss and decision capacity bottlenecks at top level. The situation tends to dictate action authority and responsibility in the organic system, whereas in the mechanistic system action authority responsibility is pre-programmed.

Therefore the organic/mechanistic dimension runs from *B* to *B'* in Fig. 8.1 in the direction of increasing technological change. It describes an additional spectrum of internal organisational forms to the M-form, U-form dimension.

In practice we would expect four extreme polar types of internal organisation; functional/mechanistic, functional/organic, divisional/

mechanistic, divisional/organic. The precise form adopted will depend on degree of activity relatedness and environmental technological change. The functional/divisional spectrum describes the alternatives for organising groups within the organisation; the mechanistic/organic spectrum describes the decision-making processes of these groups. Therefore, the context in which mechanistic/organic systems operate is set by the functional/divisional spectrum. For example a firm may adopt a project team approach based on organic system principles, but it will do so within the context of a functional or divisional organisational form.

Therefore we have established expectations as to nature of the internal organisation form adopted by firms operating within the boundaries of the box diagram of Fig. 8.1. However we have previously argued that firms operating in that box diagram will adopt

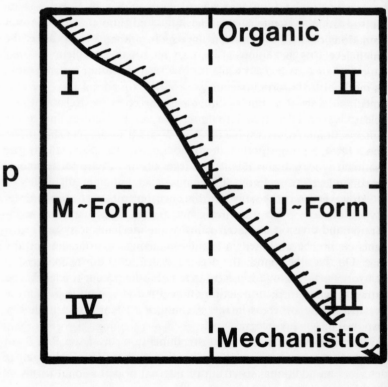

FIGURE 8.2. Strategy and structure

strategies consistent with the level of technological change in their environment; environment determines strategy. Chandler (1966), Williamson (1970 and 1975) and Ansoff (1965) have also argued that strategy determines structure, as was discussed at the start of the chapter. We have further argued here that environment directly determines another element of structure (mechanistic/organic spectrum). In the next section we shall attempt to demonstrate the existence of order in this apparent mish-mash of environment, strategy and structure relationships.

STRATEGY AND STRUCTURE

The relationship between strategy and structure is demonstrated by overlaying Fig. 5.5 on Fig. 8.1 to construct Fig. 8.2, in which the introduction of strategic considerations indicates that certain combinations of organisation forms are more probable than others. For high levels of technological change, an organic M-form system is appropriate (quadrant I) while for low levels of technological change, a mechanistic U-form system is appropriate (quadrant III). For intermediate levels of technological change the correct association is less clear; we have contrived to make the survival constraint cut the intersection point separating the four organisational types, but there is no a *priori* reason why this should be the case. Consequently, organisational types associated with quadrants II or IV may occur at intermediate levels of technological change.

However we can go further than just indicate preferred structure types; we can identify environment/strategy/structure relationships from Fig. 8.2. A high level of environmental technological change encourages a strategy with a low degree of activity relatedness and an organic system approach; the corporate strategy encourages an M-form structure. A technologically stable environment encourages a strategy with a high degree of activity relatedness, and a mechanistic system approach; the strategy encourages a U-form structure. Thus we have a technological change/diversification/M-form/organic system association and a stable technology, specialisation/U-form/ mechanistic system association. Intermediate levels of technological change should be associated with appropriate intermediate stages for each of the other three dimensions. We can summarise these relations in Fig. 8.3. Environment is the determinant of strategy and choice of organic or mechanistic system, as indicated by lines (a) and (b) respectively. Strategy determines choice of M-form or U-form corporation as indicated by line (c). This last connection is the strategy/ structure relationship identified by Chandler, Williamson and Ansoff.

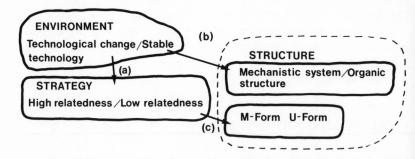

FIGURE 8.3   Environment, strategy, structure

We have already examined relation (a) in previous chapters, and our findings tend to support this hypothesised relationship. Technological change tends to be associated with a strategy of low activity relatedness, and stable technology tends to encourage a strategy of high activity relatedness.

As far as relation (b) is concerned, the limited empirical evidence available tends to support the hypothesised relationship. In a comparison of electronics firms, Burns and Stalker (1961) found that firms which had adopted an organic type of structure tended to perform better than firms which utilised a mechanistic approach. This suggests that the organic system is more appropriate to technologically dynamic environments. Subsequently, Hage and Aiken (1969) studied a number of health and welfare agencies which varied widely in the degree of routineness of tasks performed; organisations with routine work were more likely to be associated with centralisation of authority and power, compared to organisations which dealt with comparatively non-routine and varied work. This is consistent with agencies dealing with routine work adopting a mechanistic system.[2]

The third relation (c) has received a good deal of attention in recent years. For his sample of large US corporations, Rumelt (1974) found a relationship between structure and diversity that was statistically significant at the 1 per cent level; functional corporations had an average specialisation ratio of .811, functional with subsidiaries (a mixed or intermediate form) had an average specialisation ratio of .675, and product division corporations had an average specialisation ratio of .469. If strategic categories instead of specialisation ratios were used to predict structural form, predictive ability improved even further (p.74). Dyas and Thanheiser (1976) also found that strategy determined structure for their sample of large French and German firms, as did Channon (1973) for UK firms.

Therefore, the available evidence to date tends to support the environment/strategy/structure relationships hypothesised in Fig. 8.3. This is in turn consistent with the integration of strategy and structure in Fig. 8.2

CONTROL LOSS AND INTERNAL TRANSACTION COSTS

One aspect of internal organisation deserves further attention. In the analysis so far we have identified two costs of co-ordinating inter-group decision-making within the firm; control-loss and internal transaction costs. Depending on the context they have both been identified as costs of inter-group co-ordination; Williamson's analysis emphasises the former, our analysis has tended to favour internal transaction costs while recognising the possible importance of control-loss in hierarchical co-ordination.

These costs are a reflection of alternative methods of inter-group co-ordination. We demonstrate this is Fig. 8.4. *A* and *E* are two groups (say divisions) which have a strong link (say shared market). Now, if co-ordination of market synergy is carried out by inter-group transactions (indicated by the dotted line *A* to *E*), we are liable to encounter internal transaction costs of the type discussed earlier. If, on the other hand, co-ordination of market synergy is carried out by hierarchical co-ordination with *C* as peak-co-ordinator, then we face

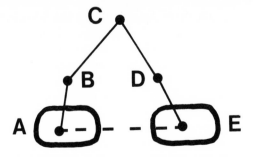

FIGURE 8.4   Hierarchy: control-loss and internal transaction costs

control-loss problems from transmission of information A to C and E to C via the respective intermediaries B and D.

Therefore control loss and internal transaction costs reflect differences in methods of co-ordinating inter-group links, and may be regarded as alternative costs of organisation. Both increase with increases in inter-group links; if we wished the analysis of internal organisation in Chapter 3 could have been carried out with control-loss substituting internal transaction costs as the source of inefficiency in inter-group co-ordination.[3] Which loss obtains depends on whether and how authority is centralised or delegated.

CONCLUSION

This has been a short chapter but it is nevertheless an important one since it has developed an integrated approach to strategy and internal organisation. While such in integration has been suggested before, it has typically been concerned with the direct relations between strategy and U-form/M-form structures. Here we suggest that environmental technological change is the root source of strategy and structure, and interpret internal organisation in two-dimensional terms. Fig. 8.2 encapsulates the framework for the resource allocation and internal organisation relationships analysed in this chapter and the preceding two chapters.

It is interesting that both dimensions of organisational structure are explicable in terms of decision costs and therefore can be analysed in economic terms. It is also noteworthy that the two dimensions that determined corporate strategy (activity relatedness as source of synergy, technological change as source of hedging) also determine internal organisation (activity relatedness for the M-form/U-form spectrum, technological change for the mechanistic/organic spectrum). The consequence is that Fig. 8.2 displays an attractive symmetry in its representation of strategy and structure relationships.

9 Concluding Remarks

The purpose of this work has been to suggest how structuralism may contribute to economics. It is built on the strong conviction that the dominance of techniques based on aggregation in economics has had a deleterious effect on the adequacy of theory building. Non-decomposable systems will always resist understanding and explanation if viewed through the distorting lens of aggregation. The solution is to change the lens, not to distort the view.

In recent years economics has been bedevilled by the elaboration and refining of irrelevant theories. Pareto efficiency is an obsession with micro-economists, and the refining of welfare theory invoking this utopian ideal is a pursuit favoured by many of the most able and powerful economic theorists; but then again, the Philosopher's Stone was an obsession with chemists in the Middle Ages and the refining of material in search of this magical catalyst was a pursuit much favoured by many of the most able chemists. Obsession does not legitimate misdirected effort.[1] The development of high theory such as that exemplified by the mathematical general equilibrium theorists does not add to our understanding of how things work, and is not justifiable on positive grounds. Nor is it justifiable on normative grounds since understanding must precede policy. High theory based on flimsy foundations must be at best a shaky edifice. At worst it is unscientific to the extent that it divorces itself from the iterative relationship between theorising and empirical observation.

The theory developed here is built on simple structuralist foundations. The firm is fashioned out of synergy and the threat of environmental change. Transaction costs, particularly bounded rationality and opportunism result in the firm supplanting the market as a mode of conducting transactions. In the absence of transaction costs, there is no reason why in general the market could not organise the exploitation of synergy; transaction costs create the multi-product firm. These points constitute the basis for our structuralist interpretation of the firm.

However, although we have looked at a wide variety of problems in this work, it may reasonably be asked how general this approach is. We shall consider this problem in the next section before going on to suggest how it may be placed in the context of microeconomics and related areas.

GENERALITY OF THE APROACH AND POSSIBLE DIRECTIONS OF FUTURE RESEARCH

There are areas studied here for which it might be easier to claim adequate explanation than for others. The recent evolution of the large highly diversified unrelated or related-linked corporation parallels the development of improved information and analysis at firm and industry level. These factors combine to support confidence in our explanation of corporate strategy and diversification in Chapter 6. Similarly, the evolution of organic and multidivisional organisation forms are fairly recent phenomena and the predicted meshing of strategy and structure appeared well supported by empirical analysis, though in a piecemeal fashion; the individual relations composing the total perspective on strategy/structure as outlined in Chapter 8 have been examined one at a time rather than within an overall framework.

However, some of the issues discussed in Chapter 7 are less straight-forward. Firstly, analysis of changes in industry concentration were carefully selected for a particular time period and a restricted industry band (3–4 digit level). Secondly, the merger wave of the post-war period is not unique; in the case of the US there were two significant merger waves at the start of the twentieth century and during the late twenties (Reid, 1968, p.15). Finally, there have been continuing changes in overall concentration over a long period; there appears to have been a general though erratic upwards trend since the early twentieth century for the US (see Blair, 1972, p.63).

As far as the changes in industry concentration are concerned, similar results may be expected elsewhere, or it may be a special case reflecting the conditions of rapidly accelerating technological change in the early post-war period. The changes in overall concentration are consistent with a continuing process of accelerating technological change over the twentieth century, though of course simple growth of markets over this long time period would also facilitate diversified strategies through creation of extra market room without necessarily leading to changes in aggregate concentration.

The other phenomenon which has a long standing history is merger waves. In this connection there appears to be a significant relationship between stock market conditions and merger activity (Maule, 1968). However our explanation is devoid of financial market considerations. Are these differing viewpoints reconcilable? Nelson (1959, p.125) provides relevant comment:

> It is possible that merger movements represent a burst of industrial reorganisation toward which underlying economic and technological developments have been accumulating a long time. A favourable capital market may, under these circumstances, trigger the massive reorganisation. Thus while the findings of (this) study may have demonstrated clearly the importance of the capital market as a proximate factor in merger movements, they have not so clearly demonstrated its importance as an ultimate cause.

Further research is required to consider the interplay, if any, between financial and industrial considerations, shareholder and managerial objectives, and merger activity. However, the delayed appearance of conglomerate merger until the post-war period is consistent with a pattern of synergy-rich mergers pre-war and increased hedging post-war, as we would expect from our analysis. To what extent financial stimulus must augment technological stimulus requires further investigation.

There is also an area which has been neglected in this study, and that is the role of the small firm. For the UK, Amey (1964) found that degree of diversification was strongly related to size of firm, and Gort (1966) found similar results for the US. Our analysis is designed for large firms and does not appear to have immediate application for small firms.

In fact small firms are liable to face strong competing motives of synergy and hedging. Design and choice of strategy may be a luxury that the small firm cannot afford. The strategy dictated by the survival constraint may be unattainable without sacrificing a great deal of synergy; in the limit the small firm may concentrate on a single product-market to exploit economies of scale. We may integrate the small firm into the analysis by imputing a growth motive with attainment of the survival constraint as an objective. Alternatively, the model may be made general by recognising that catastrophe potential may not simply operate as a constraint, but may be traded off against profitability, explicitly recognising that for small firms hedging may have very high opportunity costs in terms of synergy. The surprising feature of the extremely simple model developed in Chapter 5 is that it took our analysis as far as it did; we would expect future developments to extend its scope and generality. In this respect, synergy/hedging trade-off is an obvious reason for the higher level of specialisation of small firms in general.

A further area of related interest is that of vertical integration. Williamson (1975) conducts a comprehensive analysis of this area based on a transaction cost approach. Williamson's analysis of vertical integration in terms of internalising the incremental transaction is mirrored in our comparison of firm versus market exploitation of synergy. Further research may help to highlight further the common transaction cost underpinnings of both vertical integration and diversification.

The point at which the analysis stops is at tactical level, or at the level of the individual product. We have totally ignored tactical problems so far, and in the next section we indicate how strategy and tactics complement each other. The potential scope of our approach is as wide as industrial organisation, though some problems must be regarded as essentially tactical.

THE THEORETICAL FRAMEWORK

At an early stage in our analysis we introduced the concepts of synchronic and diachronic relations. These constituted essential foundations for our later analysis. Although economic theory is generally quite explicit in distinguishing static from dynamic, a central argument here is that this is not sufficient; the question of relations between elements in static and dynamic analysis is also important. In particular, the ignoring of synchronic relations in the theory of the firm was identified as a serious omission.

Seen from the point of view of traditional theory, synchronic relations signal non-decomposable systems, serve to confuse orderly analysis, and interfere with basic assumptions. It is convenient to assume they do not exist. However, from a structuralist perspective these relations form an integral part of system description. Rather than pretend they are not there, structuralism recognises the centrality of synchronic relations.

The structure of the firm is held together by transaction costs, Coase's (1937) and Simon's (1961) analyses has been integrated and further developed into a transaction cost analysis of the firm by

Williamson. Williamson (1975) is the fullest expression of this development. However this work is mostly concerned with detailed consideration of single product problems (vertical integration) and decomposable systems (conglomerates). The purpose of this work has been to demonstrate the potential of a structuralist approach to non-decomposable multiproduct firms. Synergy is a major payoff for the multiproduct firm, and transaction costs are the sticking plaster that bind together the synergy-seeking multiproduct firm.

The other payoff pursued by the multiproduct firm, hedging, is the converse of synergy. It is an attempt by the firm's management to ensure continuing future employment in the fact of transient product viability. It emphasises product life cycle considerations and may be said to have Schumpterian origins;[2] hedging is an aspect of strategy which attempts to counter the threat to corporate survival posed by the process of creative destruction. While synergy is based on links between activities, hedging is based on their absence; further, while synergy is synchronic, hedging is based on diachronic relationships. The nature of the environment is the factor which determines the appropriate balance of synergy and hedging.

The relationship between strategy and structure (or internal organisation) is also determined by transaction costs. A contribution made here is to suggest that not only may bounded rationality and opportunism decide whether transactions are carried out intra-firm or by the market but that these same transaction costs may decide organisation form. Again, non-decomposability is fundamental; it was argued that control-loss problems and internal transaction costs both derive directly from this condition. Control-loss and internal transaction costs obtain from attempts to exploit potential links between different groups in the firm, and co-ordinate the division of labour. Complete decomposability eliminates the need for hierarchical or inter-group co-ordination and eliminates these sources of inefficiency.

It is suggested here that non-decomposability is the natural condition of large firms and should not be regarded as a symptom of eccentric or deviant systems. A useful aspect of widening our perspective to include the application of structuralism to other social sciences has been the demonstration that non-decomposability can be a starting point for analysis, not an insuperable barrier. However, this is a distinctive and indeed contrary viewpoint to that provided by received microtheory. In the next section we shall discuss further how this approach stands in relation to conventional theory.

CONTEXT

The approach developed here may be nominated as a complement or an alternative to other approaches, depending on specific circumstances. We shall consider both theoretical and empirical possibilities in turn.

Firstly, the immediate theoretical frame of reference of this work is the theory of the firm, while microeconomic theory as a whole provides a broader context against which the approach may be set. On the applied side, industrial organisation is the empirical area in economics of concern here, while business policy is an area of normative investigation which may benefit from the analytical framework developed earlier.

1 *Theory of the Firm*

The neoclassical theory of the firm is built around single product analysis. In one respect it may be regarded as a special case of the approach developed here in which synergy links between all units of output are perfect or complete; synergy becomes economies of scale.

However its emphasis on competitive considerations such as barriers to entry, technological effects in cost curves, demand conditions, is a complement to the structuralist approach. We have emphasised environment and product-market links as a determinant of strategy in our analysis; neoclassical theory emphasises cost and revenue conditions for a specific product-market as a determinant of tactics. The integration of strategy and tactics within an overall battleplan for the firm is an obvious and natural development. A qualification is in order; even in the area of tactics, a neoclassical analysis may prove inferior to a transaction cost analysis (see Williamson, 1975, pp.205–1).

As far as the more recent managerial theories of the firm are concerned, these may also be integrated with our analysis in future. In pursuing profits, we leave open the question of whether these profits are an end in themselves, or a means to an end. They may be used to fund managerial emoluments, investment for growth, dividends, or other objectives.[3] Any integration, if carried out, would be performed within a global structuralist perspective. Such a perspective is already explicit in Marris (1971) in which determinants of the operating profit rate are analysed, and then the global relationship between profit and growth analysed *after* the profit rate has been determined. This represents an abandonment of the elegant, though sterile, simultaneity associated with general equilibrium theory. The hierarchic ordering of relationships is perfectly natural in a structuralist approach, but is not analysable within the aggregative world of simultaneous relationships associated with general equilibrium theory. In Kay (1979), a similar global approach to the question of tradeoffs between resource allocations to R & D and production/marketing was advocated. It may also be possible to integrate this approach with the analytical structuralist framework of the present work.

In this connection one further point relating to the analysis of previous chapters merits discussion. In Chapter 4 we discussed two mixed forms in Fig. 4.5 (firm Chi) and Fig. 4.6 (firm Pi) in which hybrid organisation structures resulted from technological synergy and market synergy respectively. The former case corresponds to Marris's transcendent corporation while the latter has an analogous organisation structure, though sales replaces R & D as the separate function.

While this must be a tentative hypothesis, it is suggested here that Marris's transcendent corporation is a more likely organisation form than is the analogous form represented by firm Pi. The reason for this is that R & D is likely to be a strategic device actively modifying and augmenting the product mix,[4] while the sales function is more likely to be a tactical tool specific to individual activities (as marketing implies markets). While strong synergy links may still prompt organisation forms like firm Pi, it is felt here that the form in which Marris's specifies his transcendent corporation is more probable.

2 *Microtheory*

If we view this approach in the broader context of microeconomics, an interesting parallel appears in the realm of the 'new' demand theory originally developed by Lancaster (1966, 1971, 1975). Lancaster identifies *characteristics* of goods as the basic unit of analysis; the consumer maximises his satisfaction by maximising the utility derived from bundles of characteristics provided by different goods. Goods differ in the extent to which they embody alternative characteristics and the consumer adjusts consumption accordingly to maximise satisfaction given relative prices and a budget constraint.

The important point here is that Lancaster's approach is more microanalytic than conventional product-based demand theory. In this respect it is similar to the approach developed here; while we identify shared constituents as the basic unit of analysis, Lancaster identifies common characteristics as the basis of his aproach. The analysis then procedes differently in the respective cases, but the micro-foundations are similar. Whether these parallels are a mere coincidence, or whether they may have deeper implications, is a question for further analysis.

3 *Industrial Organisation*

Insofar as the dominant structure–conduct–performance approach to industrial organisation is an applied version of neoclassical theory, the remarks made with respect to neoclassical theory in the earlier section generalise to this approach. The structure–conduct–performance approach is a theory of tactics, not strategy.

While a study of tactics is interesting in its own right, it is a narrow and incomplete study which should be complemented by strategic analysis if it is wished to claim any measure of generality. Further, as with neoclassical theory, even in analysis of tactics transaction cost analysis may provide an alternative approach.

4 *Business Policy*

An unexpected spin-off from the approach developed here is that it may provide a framework for business policy. Business policy is an interdisciplinary approach which is typically concerned with systematic examination of strengths/weaknesses, opportunities/ threats associated with corporate strategy. Ansoff (1965 and 1969) provides well developed and central examples of this approach.

Further development of the concept of synergy maps may provide strategy formulators with a useful tool analogous to war game models. The possible relationship between internal organisation and strategy may also become clearer if a systematic mapping of synergy links is carried out for individual firms.

We can further demonstrate how the use of synergy maps can be developed for use in the area of business policy with the aid of Fig. 9.1. One modification made below is that if a single link exists between a number of activities then it is indicated by a specific continuous bond rather than by exhaustive illustration of all possible multilateral relationships. For example, Tom Ltd in Fig. 9.1 is a related-constrained strategy with a common technological link running through all activities. If we were to identify all possible links

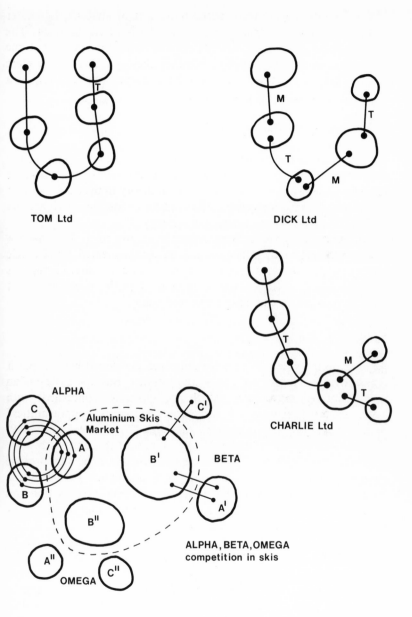

FIGURE 9.1   Alternative synergy maps

as for Alpha in Fig. 3.6 there would be 15 bonds between divisions. Add further bonds and the result would be a confusing mish-mash of divisional relationships.

However, if we adopt the convention that single link is illustrated in synergy maps by a continuous line as for Tom Ltd, then synergy maps become less complex and more comprehensible as a result. By way of contrast, Dick Ltd. operates a related-linked strategy around a series of different links as indicated by breaks or discontinuities in the lines between divisions. Charlie Ltd has a more complex strategy than either Tom or Dick since it has a single technological link between four divisions and two other minor links, one market and one technological.

Fig. 9.1 also demonstrates a simple map of a specific battleground — Alpha, Beta and Omega in the aluminium ski market. Maps like this may help to demonstrate strategic considerations, such as Omega's ability to operate B'' as a profit centre and Alpha's and Beta's greater potential for synergy gains for this market (but greater vulnerability to external threat), etc. Two other points are worth mentioning here: firstly, there may be a distinction between potential and actual synergy – a frequent observation in the business policy literature is that not all possible synergy is exploited, particularly in the area of mergers; secondly, after a point there may be synergy diseconomies in analogous fashion to diseconomies of scale. Sheer size may lead to control loss problems in exploitation of synergy, and increasing costs may result. With these extensions, synergy maps may prove to be a useful basis for examining the strengths, weaknesses, opportunities and threats of individual corporations.

CONCLUSIONS

It is not intended here to go over all the ground of this work. What has been attempted is to develop a structuralist perspective on the theory of the firm and industrial organisation. The basic standpoint of the work is the same as in Kay (1979); that aggregation in the theory of the firm distorts and misrepresents the true nature of behaviour at this level. As in that approach, a structuralist approach has been developed, though it is what is described by Piaget (1968) as an analytical structuralist approach, compared to the global structuralist approach of the earlier work.

The approach here has drawn on the concept of synergy developed by Ansoff (1965) and married it with a transaction cost analysis which has been refined and developed recently by Williamson (1975). The simple model built on these foundations has been productive and the potential for future development is significant. It is suggested as both a part substitute and part complement of existing approaches. The future scope of transaction cost analysis is one of the most interesting questions in microeconomics.

Notes and References

CHAPTER 1 INTRODUCTION

1. Behavioural theory is a notable exception, as we shall see later in the chapter.
2. However three central props of our framework merit special mention here; Piaget (1968), Ansoff (1965) and Williamson (1975). Each work is built around a major core concept (structuralism in Piaget's work; synergy in Ansoff's; and transaction cost analysis in Williamson's case) each of which will form a central element in our later analysis.
3. Hicks (1939, pp.83–5) believed that abandonment of perfect competition would lead to the wreckage of most of general equilibrium theory since stability conditions become indeterminate under monopoly. Recently Arrow (1971(b)) has demonstrated the existence of general equilibrium solution for monopolistically competitive economy. However, perfect competition still greatly eases the problems of general equilibrium analysis.
4. By 'neoclassical theory' is meant profit maximising theories including perfect competition, imperfect/monopolistic competition, monopoly and oligopoly.
5. See, for example, Koutsoyiannis (1979) for a summary of these developments.
6. In this respect, some questions have been raised with regard to the status of behavioural theory *qua* theory, since it is difficult to generalise beyond cases due to the specificity of knowledge and experience to individual firms in this approach.
7. For a discussion of this and later points made in this connection, see Bernstein (1973, pp.153–5).
8. Einstein's widely quoted phrase, '(God) does not play dice (with the universe)' – Bernstein, 1973, p.154 – summarises his attitude to the implications of quantum mechanics.

CHAPTER 2 SYSTEMS AND STRUCTURE

1. There are a number of alternative approaches in this category, including games theory.
2. See, for example, Crew, 1975, p.117.
3. Leach, 1974, pp.14–15 and p.120, note 1, provides a useful reminder that interpretations of structuralism are subject to strong debate amongst

proponets and that interpretations (including Piaget's) can be individualistic.

4. In talking of 'the conventional economic approach', in principle we include managerial theories of the firm in this category. In practice, for the reasons discussed above, we mean the traditional consumer theory and neoclassical theories of the firm of the type outlined in Henderson and Quandt (1971).

5. For a criticism that this interpretation is too simplistic, see Lévi-Strauss, 1963, p.89.

6. By behaviourism, we mean the psychological school associated with Watson and Skinner among others. This clarification is made necessary by the confusing tendency of some recent references in the theory of the firm to describe Cyert and March's behavioural theory as 'behaviourism'.

7. Modern developments in behaviourism have been characterised as S–O–R theory with O standing for organism. This is because the manner in which the organism processes information has become recognised as a central concern.

8. This was a major reason for the approach to behavioural theory adopted in Kay (1979).

9. I am grateful to Alec Vass, Department of Physics, Heriot-Watt University for this way of expressing the differences in approach.

10. At this point Hayek is comparing his interpretation with Koestler's in 'The Act of Creation'.

CHAPTER 3   THE NATURE OF THE FIRM

1. George, 1974, p.39.
2. Berry, 1975.
3. George, 1972, pp.353–68.
4. Amey, 1964.
5. Channon, 1964.
6. Prais, 1976, p.8.
7. Amey, 1964, p.265.
8. Hay and Morris give an example; Sic 3672, or 'Other radio, radar and electronics capital goods' includes 'manufacturing radio and television transmitters, radio communication receivers, radar and electronic navigational aids, high-frequency heating apparatus, magnetic compasses and gyroscopes, X-ray apparatus and electro-medical equipment (which includes infra-red, ultra-violet, radiant heat, etc., lamps for diagnosis and therapy; electrical and electronic equipment for stimulation and massage; heart, kidney, and lung machines; sterilizing equipment and reading aids).' (Hay & Morris, 1979, p.241).

9. The evaluation of individuals in professional team sports is an example of this.

10. Williamson argues that large numbers will eliminate opportunistic advantages since at the contract renewal stage traders will now agree exchanges in which competitive terms are arranged. On the other hand, small numbers enable misrepresentation and haggling.

11. Indeed it could be argued that it may increase the quality of decision making in certain cases by reducing the potential for confusion created by bounded rationality.

12. Williamson (p.46) points out the number of channels in an all-channel network is $N(N-1)/2$ (where N is number of participants) while it is only $N-1$ in the case of a peak co-ordinator.

13. While recognising that technological non-separabilities may be an important reason for the initial formation of simple task groups, Williamson discounts the relevance of Alchian and Demsetz's analysis to the issues associated with the formation of complex hierarchies (pp.49–51).

14. Although the term was used more or less casually in the business literature before Ansoff's work, Ansoff produced the first rigorous examination of the concept an its implications. Unfortunately, subsequent application of the concept by other writers has been typically characterised by a reversion to loose analysis.

15. Recently a number of papers have appeared in leading journals on the topic of economics of scope. It has been defined by Willig (1979):

> Economies of scope arise from inputs that are shared or utilized jointly without complete congestion. The shared factor may be imperfectly divisible so that manufacture of a subset of the goods leaves excess capacity in some stage of production. Or some human or physical capital may be a public input which, when purchased for use in one production process, is then freely available to another. (p.346)

> Baumol (1977) comments that that for economies of scope 'the initial concept is ... strict subadditivity of the cost function, meaning that the cost of the sum of any m output vectors is less than the sum of the costs of producing them separately'. (p.801)

> Baumol, Bailey and Willig (1977), Baumol and Braunstein (1977), and Baumol and Fischer (1978) explore the concept further and analyse its implications for multiproduct operations.

> Though none of the papers refers to synergy there is no effective distinction between the earlier concept and economies of scope. Also the papers are still rooted in a neoclassical philosophy as indicated by the specific issues studied, such as market structure and natural monopoly.

16. See, for example, Wood (1971) p.447, Melnik and Pollatschek (1973) pp.1263–73, Bridge and Dodds (1978) pp.32–3.

17. B.J. Loasby has suggested this negative synergy may be termed 'allergy'.

18. Both examples of sales synergy suggested for the tennis racquet firm may be obtainable by this method. For example the increased productivity of the ski sales force (now selling tennis racquet also) should be reflected in commission payments being low relative to the costs of employing own sales force. Also there may be 'image' or reputation benefits through marketing association with skis. However to the extent that these 'image' gains require incorporation within one firm, they are only partially appropriable through market transactions. Therefore the synergy benefits of corporate image may be partly expressable as marketing non-separabilities in analogous fashion to Alchian and Demsetz's technological non-

separabilities.

I am extremely grateful to Geoff Wyatt of the Department of Economics, Heriot-Watt University, who first raised the question of whether or not synergy could be traded, in a seminar I gave to that department. This stimulated consideration of the circumstances under which synergy could be traded, and led naturally to a consideration of the role of transaction costs.

19. As in the case of Ansoff's treatment of synergy, Clausewitz was not the first to make the distinction between strategy and tactics. However, as with Ansoff, Clausewitz provided the first rigorous analysis and development of the concepts, and provided a sound foundation for subsequent analysis.

20. Williamson's orientation tends to be concentrated on vertical integration and conglomerate organisation; 'vertical integration is...to be understood mainly as an internal organisation organisational response to the frictions of intermediate product markets, in which bounded rationality and opportunism are again prominently featured, while conglomerate organisation is interpreted as a response to (remediable) failures in the capital market, in which these very same human factors appear. albeit that the context differs'. (1975, p.56).

Since it is concerned with one final product-market, vertical integration is a tactical problem, while conglomerate organisation is easily decomposed (e.g. for control purposes). Although the multiproduct firm is analysed in Chapter 8 of Williamson's work, the role of synergy is underemphasised, separability and decomposability conditions (e.g. in the form of quasi-autonomous profit centre status of divisions) emphasised. Consequently synchronic considerations are largely ignored except for the limited role of headquarters in overview of diversification and acquisition activities.

CHAPTER 4   TECHNOLOGICAL CHANGE AND INTERNAL INTERNAL ORGANISATION

1. That is, incorporate at least some unique characteristics, or combine existing characteristics in a unique way.

2. It is assumed (p.110) that actual or potential competition encourages utility maximisation expressed solely in terms of survival potential. This survival potential is obviously facilitated by profits and diminished by losses; the reason it was decided to term the approach as utility maximising rather than profit maximising is that the latter concept is associated with the product based neoclassical approach; it was thought desirable to emphasise the break with this tradition. Further, we can explicitly associate utility with survival potential rather than a particular form of profit maximising theory, and also by using utility we do not require that a specific resource allocation has to be expressable in precise revenue and cost terms; instead management subjectively analyses and compares combinations, and chooses the combination that appears to provide the correct balance on the basis of experience, without having to quantify in detail.

3. Specifying the preference system in terms of resources helps to avoid some

severe theoretical and empirical problems associated with product/project preference systems; for example, R & D resources are (in principle) replicable and homogenous, whereas R & D projects (by definition) are not. These properties, or their approximation, facilitate the development of definite, stable preference systems for corporate resources.

4. However, while the basis of the decision is similar in both cases, the objectives are different, being growth in Marris' theory, and survival in Kay (1979).

5. 'Negative feedback is informational input which indicates that the system is deviating from a prescribed course and should readjust to a new steady state. . . . Management is involved in interpreting and correcting for this information feedback.' (Kast and Rosenzweig, 1974, p.117).

6. It was concluded later in the work that in the light of empirical evidence (pp.168–70), stable and well established preference systems are more likely to obtain at higher levels in the firm, and that in particular, identifying an indifference curve system in quadrant 4 is possibly over-optimistic.

7. In the normal course of events, this constraint will change slowly over time, depending on the fortunes of the firm. However merger, takeover or large scale divestment may occasion substantial switches in the constraint. These are regarded here as infrequent occurrences, contingent on significant environmental opportunities or threats. As we shall see, theory based on synergy maps may provide a useful basis for analysis of these issues, but our central concern will remain the underlying reasons for the present constitution of the firm.

8. Further, since divisionalisation is by product or region, profit performance can be monitored and rewarded/penalised at this level. Such controls are difficult if not impossible to apply at functional level in the U-form corporation.

9. For example, slight synergy.

10. Nearly decomposable systems are ones in which the interactions among the subsystems are weak but not negligible (Simon, 1969, p.100).

11. However we do not agree with Simon's later conclusion that since, 'hierarchic system are, as we have seen, often nearly decomposable. Hence only aggregative properties of their parts enter into the description of the interactions of those parts.' (Simon, 1969, p.110). Merely because interactions are weak does not mean we can treat the system as an aggregate. For example, weak linkages allow us to decompose Alpha into functions; however those weak linkages are still established on an elbow length in-group basis, and indeed *it is difficult to conceive of Alpha as a viable entity unless these links are forged.* Alpha cannot be regarded as the sum of its sales, manufacturing and R & D subsystems; while weak linkages facilitate separation of groups or subsystems, this is *not* the same as saying separation of groups implies aggregation would provide adequate system description. In the example of Alpha, the pervasiveness of synchronic relations, both strong and weak, precludes aggregation in describing this system.

12. A complication of this structure is the problem of allocating R & D overheads in assessing operating divisions performance. Creating the

R & D team means that complete decomposability is not attained and separate profit measures for each division are difficult to compile and interpret. This hinders attainment of the strategy formulating and internal control features of M-form organisation.

13. Williamson talks in terms of 'internalising the incremental transaction' as being the basis for determining the boundaries of the firm (1975, p.118). However, if we consider diversification aspects of firm size, it seems appropriate to consider discrete bundles of transactions (e.g. deriving from synergy) as the basis for analysis rather than single transactions. In this perspective, potential transactions do not come singly but in bundles.

14. The chief executive of British Leyland motor corporation expresses precisely the problem of activity linking; 'there is an interdependence you can't ignore. You couldn't run J.R.T. (Jaguar Rover Triumph) without Austin Morris because you couldn't sustain the dealer network. Moreover there are a lot of common components. So you can't close down the loss-maker because the profitable one wouldn't continue to be profitable'. (Ball, 1978, p.62).

15. Ansoff does not appear to appreciate that this trade-off between synergy and flexibility exists; in fact he sees flexibility as an objective to be pursued along with synergy without recognising the potential conflict (e.g. see, 1965, p.118).

CHAPTER 5   CHOICE OF STRATEGY

1. See Markowitz (1952), (1959).
2. This is a standard formulation in the literature.
3. This example is adopted from Scherer (1970), pp.101.
4. Dyckman and Stekler show that if $r = 0$ and expected profit levels are identical for each plant, the coefficient of variation declines by $1/\sqrt{N}$ with increases in N, where N is number of plants in the combination (1965, p.214–18 and cited in Scherer, 1970, p.101)
5. An example of an exception to this would be the aluminium tennis racquet and ski example discussed earlier; the complementary nature of the respective seasonal cycles reduces profit variability by a greater amount than if the activities were unrelated, while synergy benefits are also obtainable.
6. Effectively this is shifting the risk onto a second party, and depends on the other party's ability to bear risk, and attitude towards risk.
7. There will be associated costs of stockholding.
8. Strictly speaking, vertical integration could also be considered in single period analysis; it is not considered in portfolio theory because exploitation of its advantages requires managerial control and intervention, and does not simply result from financial combination.
9. See Oi and Hurter (1965) for detailed discussion of some circumstances where these may be appropriate.
10. This, of course, assumes the parallel condition that disclosure of information will not be used opportunistically by the potential funder.
11. Plus any profit the capital market may be able to extract.

12. A further point worth making here is that a standard argument in portfolio theory is that optimal diversification may be achieved if returns are negatively correlated due to the associated effects on risk of the total portfolio. While this may be the case for holding of financial assets, it is less liable to be the case for corporate diversification, since there are two major cases in which negative correlations obtain. Firstly, counter-cyclical activities in the economy. If they are desirable to one firm for risk reduction purposes they will be attractive to many, with drastic effect on profitability of these activities. The process of competition will trade off risk reduction against profitability. Secondly, substitute goods. This is where identification of shared constituents is useful. Negative correlation in the fortunes of two activities may quickly be converted into a positive correlation if a third substitute is developed and creates catastrophe linking. Thus, short run negative correlations may hide serious costs to weigh against such risk reduction.

13. It should be borne in mind that we are dealing with constant risk here (by which we mean a constant coefficient of variation). An additional problem that is generally serious in the early stage of the life cycle is true or unmeasurable uncertainty. For the moment we leave this problem aside but return to it below.

14. We assume that if the constituent innovation (the catastrophe) is adopted by the firm, this effectively creates a *new* product market.

15. Gort (1966) has also questioned the worth of diversification to solve the inconvenience of uneven earnings and suggests instead that the 'risks' really worth diversifying are long-term 'risks', one of which is decline in earnings. In this context, he mentions switch to shorter-lived product lines as being important.

16. That is, in principle. In practice, the examples used by Schumpeter are frequently interpretable as constituents (see p.83–4)

17. A more sophisticated analysis would attempt to reconcile the problem of comparability by establishing criteria for ordering of strategies involving different mixes of shared constituents.

18. This is reasonable if the possibility of take-over raiders being attracted by a high level of liquid reserves is recognised. Take-over threat is dealt with by keeping liquidity at a level which may create vulnerability to a second type of threat due to technological change. Hedging is an alternative way of anticipating technological threat.

    We are not concerned here with how the firm actually dispenses its excess liquid funds; profits may be a source of founds for sub-objectives such as growth, dividends, etc. The use of the funds may differ according to circumstance.

19. This version of the utility function is the simplest possible given our analysis of potential catastrophe and synergy effects. A more complex version of the utility function was included in Kay (1978) but this encountered difficulties in obtaining determinate solutions.

20. The assumption of constant level of P may be seen to be more reasonable to the extent that firms tend to operate within 2-digit industries, and to the extent that these industries involve a family resemblance between technologies; for example, a food firm would tend to have low catastrophe

potential associated with its range of activities, while an electronics firm would have consistently high catastrophe potential for its range of activities. However, later analysis might explore the implications of recognising the possibility of mixing levels of P associated with the bundle of activities operated by the firm.

. There is a difficulty in that the process of competition may lead to a violation of $(\delta\pi^*/\delta r) > 0$ and $(\delta\pi^*/\delta p) > 0$ due to the changing level of profits along ZZ'. However it may be reasonable to maintain the assumption $(\delta\pi^*/\delta r) > 0$: holding P constant, the distinguishing features of each Srp are not individual activities but rather the combinations of activities. Therefore, for constant P modification of π^* for Srp on ZZ' through the process of competition should have an accompanying effect on other strategies within the relevant industry through the modification of profitability on individual activities that make up individual strategies.

Maintaining $(\delta\pi^*/\delta r) > 0$ means that utility may always be increased for firms operating to the left of ZZ' if they increase r (as indicated by the horizontal arrow in Fig. 5.5). This ensures that firms will be distributed along the locus of ZZ'.

. We would expect Beta-Two to be more profitable if its greater size permits exploitation of economies within divisions.

CHAPTER 6   DIVERSIFICATION STRATEGY

. The ratios for each company were calculated from quantitative and qualitative information compiled from a variety of sources; registers, annual reports, prospectuses, books and articles.

. Rumelt's assignment of links between activities was based on subjective evaluation of whether or not significant relationships existed between activites.

. This is more reasonable in the unrelated case than might appear at first sight, since 2-digit industry classification is generally broad enough to cover a variety of businesses having sufficiently weak links to merit the description 'unrelated'.

. 'Dominant-vertical firms are vertically integrated (vertical ratios of .7 or more) that produce and sell a variety of end products so that the specialisation ratio is less than .95' (Rumelt, 1974, pp.31–2). Of the 27 dominant business firms, only one paper and one furniture firm were not classified as dominant-vertical. (Rumelt, 1974, p.98).

. The single mining-metals firm is excluded from this analysis since R & D figures were not obtained from the available data.

. Indivisibilities occurring at different levels of output in the respective production stages may require an extremely large final output if potential economies of scale are to be fully exploited.

. Also, the dominant-vertical firms had the lowest average return on capital employed of any strategic category (Rumelt, 1974, p.92) Thus, profitability is low and the firms generally do not have a high level of internally generated funds for diversification purposes.

. Petroleum is an obvious exception.

9. For details of Xerox's phenomenal pattern of growth, see Rumelt, 1974, pp.97, 223−4. Xerox operates in a highly technological environment, but was a dominant product firm in 1969.

10. In distinguishing between science-based and non-science-based industries, the following industries were classed as science-based in each case; aerospace, chemicals, pharmaceuticals, engineering (light, heavy and electrical). The following industries were treated as non-science-based; food, drink, tobacco, petroleum, metals, materials and minerals, vehicles (excluding aircraft), textiles and clothing, glass, shipbuilding, paper and packaging printing and publishing.

11. Gort comments that the result means that 'diversification ... depends upon ... technical skills' (1962, p.135). Amey bases his use of the T-ratio on the fact that one reason commonly cited for the apparent growth of diversification has been the tremendous increase in the amount of *organised* research carried on within firms (1964, p.267). Wolf argues that the T-ratio is 'assumed to be a reasonable proxy for the firms accumulated useful stock of technical knowledge' (1977, p.181). Hassid states that the 'existence of highly developed skills ... makes easier the adjustment of already familiar production processes to the requirements of other industries' (1975, p.389). Gorecki argues that R & D activities are liable to throw up opportunities, many of which 'have characteristics which weigh the scales in favour of their exploitation by diversification rather than sales' (1975, p.138).

12. Sutton (1973) also argues from a behavioural standpoint that R & D staff may dominate decision-making in high technology industries. This might be expected to promote diversification as a result of R & D staff empire building and successfully pursuing their own objectives. Thus, internal R & D stimulates diversification in this view also. See Sutton (1974) and Grant (1974) for further discussion.

13. The other variables were firm sales, after tax profits and patents per scientist and engineer.

14. That firms do 'fine-tune' their strategies within industries *but* that industry effects can dominate and swamp these firm level effects, was argued for the firms R & D decision in Kay (1979, Chapter 8). Grabowski's analysis discussed here provided useful evidence in this analysis of the determinants of inventive activity in the firm. It also provides an alternative explanation of why the petroleum industry in Grabowki's analysis did not record a significant correlation between diversification and inventive activity (Kay, 1979, pp.197−203).

CHAPTER 7   AGGREGATE CONCENTRATION AND THE
            DIRECTION OF MERGER

1. The second assumption simplifies analysis since it means we can retain the existing diagram which is based around a specific ordering of industries in terms of technological change. Significant switching of relative positions over the two periods would necessitate the construction of a new diagram by shuffling the industry rankings.

2. In this respect see data provided by National Science Foundation (1966), p.61.
3. The year 1963 is taken as the end point of this trend since NSF data tends to suggest that overall R & D activity stabilised around that period (see Kay, 1979, p.150–3).
4. For the 15 major 2- and 3-digit industries for which both 1957 and 1963 NSF data is available, one industry recorded a constant level of R & D activity (fabricated metals) while one recorded a decrease in R & D activity (scientific and mechanical instruments). All others recorded an increase in R & D activity, and the Spearman rank correlation coefficient between 1957 and 1963 rankings was .93 (data from National Science Foundation, 1973, p.61).
5. The firms here are the ones that were not acquired or merged during the decade.
6. See Rumelt (1974) pp.56–7.
7. There are two other aspects of the related-linked strategy which must be taken into account in any comparison with the unrelated strategy; firstly, the linking process is a source of synergy, and secondly, the linking process creates a non-decomposable system.
   The first aspect is to the credit of the related-linked strategy compared to the unrelated strategy, while the second hampers or prevents effective application of the M-form structure with its superior strategy formulating and internal control properties.
   The relative importance of these considerations may affect choice and effectiveness of strategy, and may depend on circumstances.
8. However, it is worthwhile noting that for Aaronovitch and Sawyer's study of mergers, merger activity was concentrated in the period of the 1960s; if there is a correlation between acceleration and level of technological change, we would expect it to be more apparent for the early post-war period rather than the later post-war period which appears to be generally characterised by deceleration.
9. 'The 100 most acquisitive firms are defined as those that (i) were among the 200 largest in terms of 1962 assets; (ii) made at least two acquisitions during 1950 to 1963 of firms which each had more than $1 million in assets; (iii) absorbed firms whose assets totalled at least $15 million. Industries were limited to those (i) with 1958 shipments in excess of $100 million and (ii) with at least two acquisitions of over $1 million by the above 100 firms.' Wood (1971) p.436.
10. Chemicals standing as a science-based industry also makes it a focus for other firms wishing to pursue a hedging strategy; machinery firms made a number of moves into the chemical industry over this period. There is also the interesting case of non-science-based firms (in petroleum) making substantial moves into chemicals; however these should be regarded in general as *related* strategic moves into petrochemicals.

CHAPTER 8   STRATEGY AND STRUCTURE

1. This is not to say that mechanistic systems automatically note unusual

environmental signals quickly and efficiently. The mechanistic system may be associated with complacency and inertia, and such signals may be screened out of the system because they do not have programmed responses.

2. A recent text by Wieland and Ulrich (1976) provides a comprehensive analysis of theory and findings concerning the relationship between technology and structure (pp.74–95).

3. However, restricting the analysis in Chapter 3 to internal transaction costs may be justified on the grounds of principle as well as convenience. We may argue that control loss results from the need for hierarchical co-ordination which in turn results from inter-group transaction costs inhibiting effective management of synergy. The imposition of hierarchy (and resulting control-loss) may itself be regarded as a direct consequence of internal transaction costs.

CHAPTER 9   CONCLUDING REMARKS

1. For an account of the problems involved in welfare and general equilibrium theory, see Loasby (1976).

2. See Schumpeter (1942).

3. If we interpret profit in our objective function in Chapter 5 as *potential* profitability then we can include the staff component of Williamson's managerial utility function (Williamson, 1964) as another payoff provided by profit.

4. As is implied by Marris (1971) p.280–2.

Bibliography

Aaronovitch, S. and Sawyer, M. 1975, *Big Business* (London, Macmillan).

Adelman, M.A., 1961, 'The Anti-Merger Act 1950–60', *American Economic Review*, 51, 236–44.

Alberts, W., 1966, 'The Profitability of Growth through Merger', in Alberts, W., and Segall, J.E. (eds), *The Corporate Merger* (Chicago University Press).

Alchian, A.A. and Demsetz, H, 1972, 'Production, Information Costs and Economic Organisation', *American Economic Review* 62, 777–95

Amey, L.R., 1964, 'Diversified Manufacturing Business', *Journal of the Royal Statistical Society*, Series A, 127, 251–90.

Andrews, P.W.S., 1964, *On Competition in Economic Theory* (London, Macmillan).

Angyal, A., 1969, 'A Logic of Systems', in F.E. Emergy (ed.), *Systems Thinking* (London, Penguin Books).

Ansoff, H.I., 1965, *Corporate Strategy* (London, Penguin).

Ansoff, H.I., 1969, 'Toward a Strategic Theory of the Firm' in H.I. Ansoff (ed.), *Business Strategy* (London, Penguin) pp.11–40.

Arrow, K.J., 1962, 'Economic Welfare and the Allocation of Resources for Invention', in *The Rate and Direction of Inventive Activity* (Princeton University Press).

Arrow, K.J., 1968, 'Mathematical Models in the Social Sciences', in M. Brodbeck (ed.), *Readings in the Philosophy of the Social Sciences* (New York, Macmillan) pp.635–67

Arrow, K.J., 1971(a), *Essays in the Theory of Risk Bearing* (Chicago, Markham).

Arrow, K.J., 1971(b), 'The Firm in General Equilibrium Theory', in R. Marris and A. Wood (eds) *The Corporate Economy: Growth Competition and Innovative Potential* (London, Macmillan).

Ball, R., 1978, 'Saving Leyland is a Job for Hercules', *Fortune*, 3 July, 58–63.

Baumol, W.J., 1959, *Business Behaviour, Value and Growth* (New York, Harcourt, Brace and World).

Baumol, W.J., 1965, *Economic Theory and Operations Analysis*, 2nd edn (Englewood Cliffs, N.J., Prentice-Hall).

Baumol, W.J., 1977, 'On the Proper Cost Tests for Natural Monopoly in a Multiproduct Industry', *American Economic Review*, 67, 809–22.

Baumol, W.J., Bailey, E.E. and Willig, R.D., 1977, 'Weak Invisible Hand Theorems on the Sustainability of Multiproduct Natural Monopoly', *American Economic Review*, 67, 350–65.

Baumol, W.J. and Braunstein, Y.M., 1977, 'Empirical Study of Scale

Economies and Production Complementary: the Case of Journal Publication', *Journal of Political Economy*, 85, 1937–48.

Baumol, W.J. and Fischer, D., 1978, 'Cost Minimising Number of Firms and Determination of Industry Structure', *Quarterly Journal of Economics*, 20, 439–67.

Berle, A.A. and Means, G.C., 1932, *The Modern Corporation and Private Property* (New York, Commerce Clearing House Inc.).

Bernstein, J., 1973, *Einstein* (London, Fontana).

Berry, C.H., 1975, *Corporate Growth and Diversifiction* (Princeton University Press).

Blair, J.M., 1972, *Economic Concentration: Structure, Behaviour and Public Policy* (New York, Harcourt Brace Jovanovich).

Bond, R.S., 1974, 'A Note on Diversification and Risk', *Southern Economic Journal*, 41, 288–9.

Bradbury, F.R., Gallagher, W.M. and Suckling, C.N., 1973, 'Qualitative Aspects of the Evaluation and Control of Research and Development Projects', *R & D Management*, 3, 49–55.

Bridge, J. and Dodds, J.C., 1978, *Planning and the Growth of the Firm* (London, Croom Helm).

Burns, T. and Stalker, G., 1961, *The Management of Innovation* (London, Tavistock).

Calvin, A.D. (ed.), 1961, *Psychology* (Boston, Mass:, Allyn & Bacon)

Carter, J.R., 1977, 'In Search of Synergy: a Structure-Performance Test', *Review of Economics & Statistics*, Aug. 59(3) 279–89.

Chamberlin, E.H., 1933, *The Theory of Monopolistic Competition* (Cambridge, Mass:, Harvard Univeristy Press).

Champernowne, D.G., 1969, *Uncertainty and Estimation in Economics*, vol. 3 (Edinburgh, Oliver & Boyd).

Chandler, A., 1966, *Strategy and Structure* (New York, Doubleday).

Channon, D.F., 1973, *The Strategy and Structure of British Enterprise* (London, Macmillan).

Child, J., 1977, *Organisation: a Guide to Problems and Practice* (London, Harper & Row).

Chomsky, N., 1957, *Syntactic Structures* ('S Gravenhage, Mouton Press).

Chomsky, N., 1965, *Aspects of the Theory of Syntax* (M.I.T. Press).

Clare, J.W.H., 1963, 'Current Trends in the Organisation of Industrial Research', *Research Management*, 7, 393–406.

Clausewitz, C.V., 1968, in A. Rapoport (ed.), *On War* (London, Penguin).

Clifford, D.K., Jr, 1976, 'Managing the Product Life Cycle', in R.R. Rothberg (ed.), *Corporate Strategy and Product Innovation* (New York, Free Press) pp.26–35.

Coase, R.H., 1937, 'The Nature of the Firm', *Economica*, 4, 386–405.

Comanor, W.S., 1965, 'Research and Technical Change in the Pharmaceutical Industry', *Review of Economics and Statistics*, 47, 182–90.

Crew, M.A., 1975, *Theory of the Firm* (London, Longmans).

Cyert, R.M., and March, J.G., 1963, *A Behavioural Theory of the Firm* (Englewood Cliffs, N.J., Prentice-Hall).

Dyas, G.P., and Thanheiser, M.T., 1976, *The Emerging European Enterprise:*

Strategy and Structure in French and German Industries (London, Macmillan).

Dyckman, T.R. and Stekler, H.O., 1965, 'Firm Size and Variability', *Journal of Industrial Economics*, 13, 214–18.

George, K., 1972, 'The Changing Structure of Competitive Industry', *Economic Journal*, 82, Supplement, 353–68.

George, K., 1974, *Industrial Organisation*, 2nd edn (London, Allen & Unwin).

Gorecki, P.K., 1975, 'An Inter-industry Analysis of Diversification in the UK Manufacturing Sector', *Journal of Industrial Economics*, 26, 131–43.

Gort, M., 1962, *Diversification and Integration in American Industry* (Princeton University Press).

Gort, M., 1966, 'Diversification, Merger and Profits', in W. W. Alberts and J.E. Segall (eds), *The Corporate Merger* (University of Chicago Press) pp.31–4.

Gort, M., 1969, 'An Economic Disturbance Theory of Mergers', *Quarterly Journal of Economics*, 83, 624–42.

Grabowski, H.G., 1968, 'The Determinants of Industrial Research and Development: a Study of the Chemical, Drug and Petroleum Industries', *Journal of Political Economy,* 76, 292–306.

Grant, R.M., 1974, 'On the Theory of Diversification: a Comment', *Scottish Journal of Political Economy*, 1, 77–83.

Grant, R.M., 1977, 'The Determinants of the Interindustry Pattern of Diversification by UK Manufacturing Enterprises', *Bulletin of Economic Research,* Nov. 29(2) 84–95.

Hage, J.T. and Aiken, M., 1969, 'Routine Technology, Social Structure, and Organisational Goals', *Administrative Science Quarterly,* 14, 366–77.

Hagen, E.E., 1961, 'Analytical Models in the Study of Social Systems', *American Journal of Sociology,* 67, 144–51.

Hassid, J., 1975, 'Recent Evidence on Conglomerate Diversification in UK Manufacturing Industry', *The Manchester School of Economics and Social Studies,* 43, 372–95.

Hay, D.A., and Morris, D.J., 1979, *Industrial Economics, Theory and Evidence* (Oxford University Press).

Hayek, F.A., 1978, *New Studies in Philosophy, Politics, Economics and the History of Ideas* (London, Routledge & Kegan Paul).

Henderson, J.M. and Quandt, R.E., 1971, *Microeconomic Theory: a Mathematical Approach* (New York, McGraw-Hill).

Hicks, J.R., 1939, *Value and Capital* (Oxford University Press).

Higgins, R.C. and Schall, L.P., 1975, 'Corporate Bankruptcy and Conglomerate Merger', *Journal of Finance*, 30, 93–113.

Horne, J.C. Van, 1968, *Financial Management and Policy* (Englewood Cliffs, N.J., Prentice-Hall).

Kast, F.E. and Rosenzweig, J.E., 1974, *Organisation and Management: a Systems Approach,* 2nd edn (Tokyo, McGraw-Hill).

Kay N.M., 1978, *An Approach to Some Problems in Industrial Organisation,* Heriot-Watt University Economics Dept. discussion paper.

Kay, N.M., 1979, *The Innovating Firm* (London, Macmillan).

Knight, F.H., 1921, *Risk Uncertainty and Profit* (N.Y., Harper & Row).

Koestler, A., 1967, *The Ghost in the Machine* (London, Pan Books).

Koopmans, T.C., 1949, 'A Reply', *Review of Economics and Statistics,* 31 86–91.

Koutsoyiannis, A., 1979, *Modern Microeconomics*, 2nd edn (London, Macmillan).

Lancaster, K., 1966, 'A New Approach to Consumer Theory', *Journal of Political Economy*, 74, 132–57.

Lancaster, K., 1971, *Consumer Demand: a New Approach* (New York, Columbia University Press).

Lancaster, K., 1975, 'Socially Optimal Product Differentiation', *American Economic Review*, 66, 567–85.

Leach, E., 1974, *Lévi-Strauss* (London, Fontana).

Leibenstein, H., 1966, 'Allocative Efficiency versus X-efficiency' *American Economic Review*, 56, 392–415.

Leibenstein, H., 1969, 'Organisational or Frictional Equilibria, X-efficiency and the Rate of Innovation', *Quarterly Journal of Economics*, 83, 600–23.

Leibenstein, H., 1973, 'Competition and X-efficiency', *Journal of Political Economy*, 81, 765–77.

Lévi-Strauss, C., 1963, *Structural Anthropology* (London, Penguin).

Levy, H. and Sarnat, M., 1970, 'Diversification, Portfolio Analysis and the Uneasy Case for the Conglomerate Merger', *Journal of Finance*, 25, 795–802.

Lewellen, W.G., 1971, 'A Pure Financial Rationale for the Conglomerate Merger', *Journal of Finance: papers and proceedings,* 26, 521–37.

Lintner, J,, 1971, 'Expectations, Mergers and Equilibrium in Purely Competitive Securities Markets', *American Economic Review: papers and proceedings,* 41, 101–11.

Loasby, B.J., 1976, *Choice, Complexity and Ignorance* (Cambridge University Press).

Markowitz, H., 1952, 'Portfolio Selection', *Journal of Finance,* 7, 77–91.

Markowitz, H., 1959, *Portfolio Selection, Efficient Diversification of Investments,* (New York, Wiley).

Marris, R., 1963, 'A Model of the Managerial Enterprise', *Quarterly Journal of Economics,* 77, 185–209

Marris, R., 1966, *The Economic Theory of 'Managerial' Capitalism* (London, Macmillan).

Marris, R., 1971, 'The Modern Corporation and Economic Theory', in R. Marris and A. Wood (eds), *The Corporate Economy: Growth, Competition and Innovative Potential* (London, Macmillan) pp.270–317.

Maule, C.J., 1968, 'A Note on Mergers and the Business Cycle', *Journal of Industrial Economics*, 16, 99–105.

Melnik, A. and Pollatschek, M.A., 1973, 'Debt Capacity, Diversification and Conglomerate Mergers', *Journal of Finance,* 28, 1263–73.

Mueller, D., 1966, 'Patents, Research and Development, and the Measurement of Inventive Activity', *Journal of Industrial Economics*, 15, 26–37.

Mueller, D., 1969, 'A Theory of Conglomerate Mergers', *Quarterly Journal of Economics*, 83, 643–59.

National Science Foundation, 1963, *Research and Development in Industry 1960* (Washington, D.C.).

National Science Foundation, 1966, *Basic Research, Applied Research and Development in Industry 1963*, N.S.F., 72–300 (Washington, D.C.).

National Science Foundation, 1973, *Research and Development in Industry, 1971* (Washington, D.C.).

Nelson, R.L., 1959, *Merger Movements in American Industry, 1895–1956* (Princeton, National Bureau of Economic Research).

Nelson, R.R., 1976, 'Review of *Industrial Concentration: The New Learning*, by Goldshmid, Mann and Weston', *Bell Journal of Economics*, 7, 729–32.

Nelson, R.R., Peck, M.J. and Kalachek, E.D., 1967, *Technology, Economic Growth and Public Policy* (Washington, Brookings Institution).

Oi, W.Y. and Hurter, A.P., 1965, *Economics of Private Truck Transportation* (Dubuque, Iowa, William C. Brown).

Piaget, J., 1968, *Structuralism* (London, Routledge & Kegan Paul).

Prais, S., 1976, *The Evolution of Large Firms in Britain* (London, National Institute of Economic and Social Research).

Reekie, W.D., 1979, *Industry Prices and Market* (Oxford, Philip Allan).

Reid, S.R., 1968, *Mergers, Managers and the Economy* (New York, McGraw-Hill).

Robinson, E.A.G., 1934, 'The Problem of Management and the Size of the Firm', *Economic Journal*, 44, 242–57

Robinson, J., 1933, *The Economics of Imperfect Competition* (London, Macmillan).

Rumelt, R.P., 1974, *Strategy, Structure and Economic Performance* (Harvard Business School).

Ruttan, V., 1959, 'Usher and Schumpeter on Invention, Innovation and Technological Change', *Quarterly Journal of Economics*, 73, pp.596–606

Scherer, R.M., 1965, 'Firm Size, Market Structure, Opportunity and the Output of Patented Inventions', *American Economic Review*, 55, 1096–1125.

Scherer, F.M., 1970, *Industrial Market Structure and Economic Performance* (Chicago, Rand McNally).

Schumpeter, J.A., 1942, *Capitalism, Socialism and Democracy* (New York, Harper & Row).

Schumpeter, J.A., 1954, *Capitalism, Socialism and Democracy*, 4th edn (London, Unwin Bros.).

Shackle, G.L.S., 1967, *The Years of High Theory* (Cambridge, University Press).

Simon, H.A., 1957, *Administrative Behaviour* (New York, Macmillan).

Simon, H.A., 1961, *Administrative Behaviour*, 2nd edn (New York, Macmillan).

Simon, H.A., 1969, *The Sciences of the Artificial (M.I.T. Press)*.

Skinner, B.F., 1974, *About Behaviourism* (London, Cape).

Smith, K.V. and Schreiner, J.C., 1969, A Portfolio Analysis of Conglomerate Diversification, *Journal of Finance*, 24, 413–29.

Sraffa, P., 1926, 'The Laws of Returns under Competitive Conditions', *Economic Journal*, 36, 535–50.

Stigler, G., 1951, 'The Division of Labor is Limited by the Extent of the Market', *Journal of Political Economy*, 59, 185–93

Sutton, C.J., 1973, ' Management Behaviour and a Theory of Diversification', *Scottish Journal of Political Economy*, 20, 27–42.

Sutton, C.J., 1974, 'On the Theory of Diversification: a Reply', *Scottish Journal of Political Economy*, 21, 85–7.

Teece, D.J., 1980, 'Economies of Scope and the Scope of the Enterprise', *Journal of Economic Behaviour and Organization*, ı, 223–47.

Usher, A.P., 1954, *A History of Mechanical Inventions* (Harvard University Press).

Usher, A.P., 1955, 'Technical Change and Capital Formation', in *Capital Formation and Economic Growth* (Washington, D.C., National Bureau of Economic Research) pp.523–50.

Utton, M.A., 1969, 'Mergers, Diversification and Profit Stability', *Business Ratios* (1) 24–8.

Vining, R., 1949, 'Koopmans on the Choice of Variables to be Studied and of Methods of Measurements', *Review of Economics and Statistics,* 31, 91–4.

Weston, J.F., 1970, 'The Nature and Significance of Conglomerate Firms', *St. John's Law Review*, 44, 66–80.

Wieland, G.F. and Ulrich, R.A., 1976, *Organisation; Behaviour, Design and Change* (Illinois, Irwin).

Williamson, O.E., 1964, *The Economics of Discretionary Behaviour: Managerial Objectives in a Theory of the Firm* (Englewood Cliffs, N.J., Prentice-Hall).

Williamson, O.E., 1970, *Corporate Control and Business Behaviour* (Englewood Cliffs, N.J., Prentice-Hall).

Williamson, O.E., 1971, *'Managerial Discretion, Organisation Form, and the Multi-division Hypothesis'*, in R. Marris and A. Wood (eds), *The Corporate Economy; Growth, Competition and Innovative Potential* (London, Macmillan).

Williamson, O.E., 1975, *Markets and Hierarchies: Analysis and Antitrust Implications* (New York, Free Press).

Willig, R.D., 1979 'Multiproduct Technology and Market Structure', *American Economic Review, papers and proceedings,* 49, 346–51.

Wolf, B.M., 1977, 'Industrial Diversification and Internalisation: some Empirical Evidence', *Journal of Industrial Economics*, 26, 177–91.

Wood, A., 1971, 'Diversification, Merger and Research Expenditures: a Review of Empirical Studies', in R. Marris and A. Wood (eds), *The Corporate Economy: Growth, Competition and Innovative Potential* (London, Macmillan) pp.428–53.

Index

171